THE LIBRARY

University of Ulster at Magee

Due Back (subject to recall)

2 3 SEP 2008		
1 1 JAN 2013		

Fines will apply to items returned after due date

Culture and Conflict Resolution

CULTURE

& CONFLICT
RESOLUTION

KEVIN AVRUCH

United States Institute of Peace Press
Washington, D.C.

United States Institute of Peace
1550 M Street NW
Washington, DC 20005

First published 1998

Printed in the United States of America

The paper used in this publication meets the minimum requirements of American National Standards for Information Sciences—Permanence of Paper for Printed Library Materials, ANSI Z39.48-1984.

Library of Congress Cataloging-in-Publication Data
Avruch, Kevin.
    Culture and conflict resolution / Kevin Avruch.
      p.   cm.
    Includes bibliographical references and index.
    ISBN 1-878379-83-6. — ISBN 1-878379-82-8 (pbk.)
    1. Conflict management. 2. Culture. I. Title.
HM136.A93   1998
303.6'9—DC21

                                      98-30951
                                         CIP

For Sheila Kathleen,
ahuvah ve' mavourneen

Contents

Foreword

It hasn't always been so. But most scholars of conflict resolution and practitioners of the art of international negotiation now agree: culture matters. When it comes to trying to facilitate an end to a conflict, it is important to have some understanding of the cultures of the belligerents; such knowledge will help a negotiator determine what the parties really want (and don't want), and what they're prepared to do (and not to do). It is also important for a facilitator or mediator to recognize not only that his or her own culture is different from the belligerents', but also that this difference will influence how he or she tackles the task of reaching an agreement.

Admonitions to pay heed to culture as a factor in conflict management seem so self-evident today that it's surprising how long it took some analysts to recognize culture's role. But the follow-on step is less straightforward, and it takes us into more difficult intellectual territory. Yes, culture matters, but what exactly do we mean by "culture" in the context of conflict resolution, and how should cultural elements be dealt with?

Fortunately, we have an expert guide to lead us through this treacherous terrain. Kevin Avruch is a distinguished anthropologist; and surely no intellectual discipline has devoted more attention to culture than has anthropology. Furthermore, he has spent twenty years applying the insights of his discipline to the study and conduct of conflict resolution. But what makes Professor Avruch so invaluable as a guide is that he possesses not only the learning and sophistication to navigate through an area clogged with competing definitions and intricate concepts, but also the forcefulness, liveliness, concision, and wit to make our journey remarkably insightful and enjoyable.

Avruch begins by exposing the shortcomings of various past theories of, and approaches to, culture, and proposes an alternative conception, one that sees culture as dynamic and derivative of individual experience. The book then moves on to examine different theories and views (including "broad" and "restricted" views) of conflict resolution, and critiques those scholars who underestimate or dismiss the role of culture. After bringing culture and conflict resolution into the same frame of reference, the book examines how the former has been used, misused, or neglected by the latter. Avruch concludes by urging scholars, educators, and practitioners of conflict resolution to pursue techniques that make better and more productive use of a coherent concept of culture. His book rewards the reader's close attention with a refreshing, stimulating approach to one of the most pressing issues in the field of conflict resolution: how best to define, accommodate, and make use of culture and its varied manifestations.

At the United States Institute of Peace, culture—and, more specifically, culture's impact on negotiation—is the focus of a major, ongoing research and training initiative. The aim of our cross-cultural negotiating project is to enhance the productivity of international negotiations by analyzing the effects of cultural differences and training practitioners in negotiating approaches that minimize the distorting effects of culture. As part of this project, several in-depth, country-specific studies are either in progress (including analyses of North Korean, Japanese, and German negotiating practices) or have already been published (Jerrold Schecter's volume on *Russian Negotiating Behavior*). The Institute is also publishing a new edition of my own *Chinese Political*

Negotiating Behavior, a study originally carried out at the RAND Corporation. A broader, comparative perspective on the same topic is taken by Raymond Cohen, whose revised edition of Negotiating Across Cultures: *International Communication in an Interdependent World*, examines the conduct and outcomes of U.S. negotiations with Japan, China, Egypt, India, and Mexico. The objectives of the cross-cultural negotiating project are also advanced in several studies with a decidedly conceptual orientation, among them, John Paul Lederach's *Building Peace: Sustainable Reconciliation in Divided Societies* and, of course, this book on *Culture and Conflict Resolution*.

While scholars and students may comprise the primary audience for Lederach's and Avruch's books, diplomats and other practitioners of conflict resolution should also find them useful. After all, Lederach is himself as much a practitioner as a scholar, and Avruch has spent almost two decades helping to train future negotiators and mediators at George Mason University's Institute for Conflict Analysis and Resolution.

The United States Institute of Peace thus commends Kevin Avruch's concise but important volume to all who must wrestle with culture and cultural difference in the process of mediating, facilitating, or negotiating peaceful settlements to violent conflicts. Together with the other products of our cross-cultural negotiating project, *Culture and Conflict Resolution* represents our continuing commitment to providing scholars and practitioners, analysts and policymakers, specialists and generalists with the tools that will help them secure and support a more peaceful international environment.

Richard H. Solomon, President
United States Institute of Peace

Acknowledgments

Even a short book can be long in gestation and acquire for its author a long list of people to thank. For this author, primary among them is my friend and colleague Peter Black. Many of the ideas developed here first saw the light of day, and print, in collaboration with Peter. He has always saved me from committing to print an egregious error or three, and this book was no exception. I thank him greatly for this, and note that any errors that remain in the book are not his fault.

Two institutions, but especially the folks who populate them, also need to be acknowledged. I wrote the book while I was a senior fellow in the Jennings Randolph Program for International Peace at the United States Institute of Peace. The program brings together people from a wide variety of backgrounds—academic, diplomatic, journalistic, military, policy, and NGO—in a collegial and supportive atmosphere. Joe Klaits, director of the program, presides humanely over this mix. I want to thank my able research assistant, Mary Hope Schwoebel, and my program officer, John Crist. I came to value both of them as perspicuous readers and critics of my work, including that which ended up (at least for this project) on the cutting-room floor. Harley Balzer, Avner Cohen, Lewis Rasmussen, Ursula Tafe, and Marvin Weinbaum all contributed to the work. I thank Dan Snodderly and Nigel Quinney for shepherding the manuscript through the Press's editorial and review process. Conversations with Dick Solomon always helped sharpen my sense of what I did, and didn't, wish to convey in my usage of "culture."

Of the several anonymous readers engaged by the Press, some chose to reveal themselves (some did not); I thank them all and include them here in a list of others who read the manuscript critically and helped me to improve it: Peter Black, Ray Cohen, Tom Dietz, Lou Kriesberg, Marc Howard Ross, Rich Rubenstein, Robert A. Rubinstein, Joe Scimecca, and John Stone. I also want to acknowledge three individuals who provided crucial support at the beginning of the project: Shaul Bakhash, Marty Lipset, and Robert A. Rubinstein.

The second institution to be acknowledged is George Mason University, which, sometimes despite itself, has provided me a hospitable home for thinking, teaching, and writing these thoughts. Within my home department, Sociology and Anthropology, I am blessed with colleagues who take a very broad view of relevant research and scholarship, without preconceived ideas of what it is anthropologists are supposed to do. (Not that it would matter all that much, I suspect. A degree in anthropology is, as Clyde Kluckhohn once remarked, an intellectual poaching license in any case.) The various department chairs with whom I have worked over the years—Joe Scimecca, Peter Black, John Stone, and Lois Horton—have all striven to keep the department open and receptive in this way.

My other home at George Mason has been its Institute for Conflict Analysis and Resolution, which I helped to found in 1980. Through the years, many affiliated with ICAR have made it possible for me to teach and learn, and much of what I have taught and learned is reflected in this book. Teachers learn more than some of us would care to admit from our students, so let me acknowledge the several generations of ICAR students whom it has been my privilege to teach, and learn from. Of colleagues, I want especially to acknowledge Dan Druckman (who let me sit

ACKNOWLEDGEMENTS

in as *his* student in his Negotiation class), Chris Mitchell, Rich Rubenstein, and Dennis Sandole. Thanks go to Tom Williams, the first chair of ICAR's faculty advisory board, for inviting me to join in 1980. My several disagreements with John Burton will be obvious to even the most distracted reader of this book; I want here to acknowledge his foundational contributions to ICAR and, more profoundly, to conflict resolution. Finally, I want to recall the contributions of the late Jim Laue, and of Henry Barringer and the late Bryant Wedge, who brought the idea of what was to become ICAR to George Mason University twenty years ago.

I dedicate the book to Sheila, and through her, to Carla and Liza, too.

Culture and Conflict Resolution

Introduction

The aims of this essay are, first, to set out and explore critically the many, sometimes competing, ways in which the idea of culture has been theorized, and then to see how it has been used, or dismissed, by students and practitioners of conflict resolution. This is a moment in conflict resolution and peace research when attention is being directed to the place of culture in the discourses of practitioners and theorists. But along with the realization that culture matters has come great conceptual confusion about the term, resulting in work in the field that is less satisfactory than it should be.

The confusion arises not only from the difficulty of the term itself and from the plethora of ways in which it has been theorized and explained (or explained away) but also from the way culture has been factored into the design stage of conflict resolution processes. Partly, this confusion stems from the curious history of the term and from the varied academic disciplines that have adapted the notion to their own disciplinary idioms. In some idioms "culture" is merely a label, a handy name for persons aggregated in some social, often national, sometimes ethnic, grouping; the name given to the group distinguishes it from other such groups. In other idioms, related to the one we shall adopt, "culture" is conceived more deeply, as an evolved constituent of human cognition and social action. In some measure, too, the confusion over culture arises because the term is increasingly used in conflict situations by the parties or contestants themselves, usually as part of highly politicized and conflict-saturated discourses of identity, ethnicity, and nationalism. In fact, the ultimate usefulness of "culture" as a social science term is now threatened by its having been taken over by the political actors it is meant to explain—think, for example, of its strategic use in the human rights debate.

In part I of the essay we develop a conception of culture that, avoiding some of the inadequacies of past ways of thinking about it, gives us a framework for considering its uses in conflict resolution theory and practice. In part II we discuss different ways of theorizing social conflict, and the sorts of conflict resolution these different ways entail. In this part we also introduce the notion of two divergent views of conflict resolution, the broad and the restricted. Next, special attention is given to the role of culture in international relations theory and the practice of diplomacy. The views of "skeptics" as to the usefulness of cultural approaches, especially views representing the dominant realist paradigm in international relations, are addressed here.

Part III brings culture and conflict resolution into the same frame of reference by considering critically two strategies for understanding culture: the actor-oriented emic and the analyst-oriented etic approaches. In part IV we examine the role culture has played (or not played) in different theories and practices of conflict resolution, highlighting the development of the problem-solving workshop and addressing once again the views of some culture skeptics. This part concludes by returning to our two conceptions of conflict resolution (broad and restricted) in terms of the current state and the future of the field.

In the essay's conclusion we address practitioners and trainers/educators, those whose major concerns with conflict resolution lie not so much in theory as in practice.

Part I: Culture

In the essay's first part we develop the idea that culture is a derivative of individual experience, something learned or created by individuals themselves or passed on to them socially by contemporaries or ancestors. As we will see, such a conception of culture differs from ones that have dominated thinking in much of the social sciences, especially in international relations and conflict resolution. For one thing, in this concept, culture is seen as something much less stable or homogenous than in the concepts proposed by others. Our idea of culture focuses less on patterning and more on social and cognitive processing than older ideas of culture do. For another, by linking culture to individuals and emphasizing the number and diversity of social and experiential settings that individuals encounter, we expand the scope of reference of culture to encompass not just quasi- or pseudo-kinship groupings (tribe, ethnic group, and nation are the usual ones) but also groupings that derive from profession, occupation, class, religion, or region. This reorientation supports the idea that individuals reflect or embody multiple cultures and that "culture" is always psychologically and socially distributed in a group. Compared with the older approach, which connected a singular, coherent, and integrated culture to unproblematically defined social groups, this approach makes the idea of culture more complicated. Such complication is necessary, because the world of social action, including conflict and its resolution, is a complex one, and we need a different concept to capture it.

The Concept of Culture: A Very Brief History

We ought to begin, then, by recognizing just how difficult a concept *culture* is. Raymond Williams writes, "Culture is one of the two or three most complicated words in the English language."[1] More than half a century ago, two eminent American anthropologists, A. L. Kroeber and Clyde Kluckhohn, surveyed the field for definitions of culture and came up with more than 150 of them.[2] Much of the difficulty stems from the different usages of the term as it was increasingly employed in the nineteenth century. Broadly speaking, it was used in three ways (all of which can be found today as well). First, as exemplified in Matthew Arnold's *Culture and Anarchy* (1867), culture referred to special intellectual or artistic endeavors or products, what today we might call "high culture" as opposed to "popular culture" (or "folkways" in an earlier usage). By this definition, only a portion—typically a small one—of any social group "has" culture. (The rest are potential sources of anarchy!) This sense of culture is more closely related to aesthetics than to social science.

Partly in reaction to this usage, the second, as pioneered by Edward Tylor in *Primitive Culture* (1870), referred to a quality possessed by all people in all social groups, who nevertheless could be arrayed on a development (evolutionary) continuum (in Lewis Henry Morgan's scheme) from "savagery" through "barbarism" to "civilization." It is worth quoting Tylor's definition in its entirety, first because it became the foundational one for anthropology, and second because it partly explains why Kroeber and Kluckhohn found definitional fecundity by the early 1950s. Tylor's definition of culture is "that complex whole which includes knowledge, belief, art, morals, law, custom, and any other capabilities and habits acquired by man as a member of society."[3] In contrast to Arnold's view, all folks "have" culture, which they acquire by virtue of membership in some social group—society. And a whole grab bag of things, from knowledge to habits to capabilities, makes up culture.

The extreme inclusivity of Tylor's definition stayed with anthropology a long time; it is one reason political scientists who became interested in cultural questions in the late 1950s felt it necessary to delimit their relevant cultural domain to "political culture." But the greatest legacy of Tylor's definition lay in his "complex whole" formulation. This was accepted even by those later anthropologists who forcefully rejected his evolutionism. They took it to mean that cultures were wholes—integrated systems. Although this assertion has great heuristic value, it also, as we shall argue below, simplifies the world considerably.

The third and last usage of culture developed in anthropology in the twentieth-century work of Franz Boas and his students, though with roots in the eighteenth-century writings of Johann von Herder. As Tylor reacted to Arnold to establish a scientific (rather than aesthetic) basis for culture, so Boas reacted against Tylor and other social evolutionists. Whereas the evolutionists stressed the universal character of a single Culture, with different societies arrayed from savage to civilized, Boas emphasized the uniqueness of the many and varied cultures of different peoples or societies. Moreover he dismissed the value judgments he found inherent in both the Arnoldian and Tylorean views of culture; for Boas, one should never differentiate high from low culture, and one ought not differentially valorize cultures as savage or civilized.

Here, then, are three very different understandings of culture. Part of the difficulty in the term lies in its multiple meanings. But to compound matters, the difficulties are not merely conceptual or semantic. All of the usages and understandings come attached to, or can be attached to, different political or ideological agendas that, in one form or another, still resonate today. Arnold's sense of culture (some have it and some—most—don't) strongly implies class and other social status divisions. It can be used to separate the elite from the masses, the center from the periphery, North from South, East from West, and so on. One contemporary direct descendent of *Culture and Anarchy* is *The Dictionary of Cultural Literacy*.[4] The reactions to this prescriptive—and, it is charged, Eurocentric, sexist, or racist—construal of culture have reverberated especially strongly in the so-called canon wars of the academy. There, cultural studies arose, among other reasons, to dethrone such elitist notions of culture (or, indeed, of literacy) by, among other tactics, subverting the distinction between high and low (Tupac Shakur is the equal of Milton), or reversing their valences entirely (rap is superior to *Paradise Lost*).

The political baggage of Tylor's sense of culture (and that of the many other nineteenth-century writers of his ilk) lies in the evolutionist and developmental assumptions that were deployed with the term in his thinking and writing. The notion that some human groups were like Stone Age savages or, more generally, that all of social evolution conspired to create the nineteenth-century Church of England Oxbridge gentleman, fit very well the ideological requirements of colonialism and empire. At its most generous (attached to the idea that movement "up" the evolutionary ladder is possible for anyone, given sufficient ambition and instruction), it could underscore the "civilizing missions" of different and competing empires.

With Boas, finally, we get a view of culture set forth in opposition to both Arnold's and Tylor's views. Boas's view is classically liberal. As noted previously, Boas stressed the plurality of diverse cultures rather than their universal attributes; second, he sought to disentangle this sense of culture from ideas of race and even of language; and third, he argued for the moral equivalence of cultures. This last idea was developed especially in the writings of his prolific students—Ruth Benedict, Melville Herskovits, and Margaret Mead—into the notion of cultural relativism, which (variously construed and misconstrued) occupies its own set of bunkers in the canon wars and identity politics of contemporary public debate. With some relevance to conflict resolution issues, the relativism debate has also become connected to the discursive politics of human rights.

In sum, part of the reason for the difficulty in applying the notion of culture to conflict resolution is that the notion of culture comes to the social sciences from nineteenth-century usages with very different, indeed antithetical, meanings. Another part of the reason is that although culture is supposed to function as a technical term in the social sciences, it is burdened not only by its multiple meanings but also by its freighted political baggage. In truth, "culture" was never fully divorced from a political program of one sort or another: from Tory elitism to Kiplingesque colonialism to liberal antiracism.[5] Any contemporary use of the term must recognize and then (if one is brave enough to continue) partition out this background.[6] Finally, even when the term has been employed in its most useful form—that is, as a modified Boasian term, to be discussed below—it has been used attached to some wholly inadequate understandings of social and cognitive processes. We move to this now.

An Approach to Culture

To retain the idea of culture as an *analytical* tool we must begin by dismissing Arnold's construction of it; there is no sense in which culture is the sole possession of an educated, affluent, or highbrow few. We cannot, however, dismiss the idea that others (political actors) may hold strongly to this very view. This is less a paradox than a demonstration of the importance of the distinction between *etic* (analyst-relevant) and *emic* (actor-relevant) concepts—two terms to be dealt with in more detail later in the essay. It is also a demonstration of the constitutive power of culture to construct an emically meaningful but analytically nonveridical definition of culture.[7] This constitutive quality of culture is something we will return to again.

Having left Arnold to the players, so to speak, we move to fashion a working definition of culture for both theory and practice in conflict resolution. We said the definition must be a modified Boasian one, and that means accepting that culture will always present two faces to the analyst. One face is the universalist one of Tylor, though shorn of the teleologies of nineteenth-century evolutionist thinking. The other face is the Boasian one of particularist cultural diversity.

These two orders of culture have gone by different names. Black and Avruch refer to them respectively as *generic* and *local* culture.[8] Generic culture is a species-specific attribute of Homo sapiens, an adaptive feature of our kind on this planet for at least a million years or so.[9] Local cultures are those complex systems of meanings created, shared, and transmitted (socially inherited) by individuals in particular social groups. Generic culture directs our attention to universal attributes of human behavior—to "human nature." Local culture directs our attention to diversity, difference, and particularism. Much confusion (and academical polemic) results from ignoring one or another dimension of culture. To ignore local cultures is to rely on a theoretically overdeveloped and deterministic concept of human nature that erases the observable facts of cultural variability and in practice usually ends up meaning, as Clifford Geertz once put it, that everyone else is less well got-up editions of ourselves.[10] (Negotiation looks the same everywhere. But sometimes you just have to speak louder and slower.) But to ignore generic culture is to find oneself locked in the sealed cylinder of a postmodern solipsism—and to lose sight of the possibilities of *intertranslatability* across local cultures or, to put it at the level of individuals, of the potential for social and experiential learning.

For this essay, we will assume generic culture as foundational, for how else could cultural outsiders ever usefully intervene in a conflict in a different culture—or even hold a conversation there? Having made this assumption, we will concentrate on the implications and dynamics of local cultures—that is, on variability and diversity. But we are still left with the need for a theoretically adequate conceptualization of local culture (hereafter, simply *culture*), and this is where we must modify the older Boasian formulation. For every concept is to some extent the epistemological hostage of the discipline or discourse that gave rise to it, and for a good deal of its contemporary existence, the concept of culture was the hostage of anthropology, that is, of that discipline's traditional subject matter, research setting, and dominant methodology. The traditional subject matter of anthropology was the study of "custom"; the traditional setting, a village or small-scale community in a non-Western, tribal, or peasant setting; the dominant methodology, ethnography based on face-to-face encounters and participant-observation of contemporaneous and ongoing (real-time) social life. Each of these bound the concept of culture in characteristic ways. To study custom is to risk missing the dynamism of social relations.[11] The focus on *the* "X" or "Y" tribe often carried with it assumptions of social isolation and minimal contact between groups (or between villages with indigenous centers). The microsociological thrust of fieldwork and the temporal constraints of the "ethnographic present" could blind us to larger social, political, or economic forces, or to long-term processes of large-scale, longitudinal change (to history, in a word). Among other things, these limitations all gave rise to some fairly inadequate ideas about culture. However, within anthropology the concept of culture has been around long enough to have changed as a result of disciplinary developments, so that the concept held at the time of Mead or Benedict or Malinowski—not to mention Boas or Tylor—is not the one dominant today. But there is often a curious lag when concepts are taken from one discipline and used in the theory making of another. And so although the inadequate ideas about culture that will be discussed below are not much found in anthropology any more, they can easily be found in related disciplines that have sought to adopt and use the concept of culture—disciplines such as international relations, or quasi disciplines (and their associated emergent practices) such as conflict resolution. By way of sharpening our own conception of culture, let us examine some grossly inadequate ones.

Inadequate Ideas of Culture

For analytical purposes—for the understanding of conflict processes as well as practices of conflict resolution, in our case—a
conception of culture is *inadequate* (a) if it fails to reflect the "thick-
ness," or complexity, of the phenomenological world it seeks to
represent, that is, if it oversimplifies; or (b) if it is connected, overtly
or covertly, to a political or ideological agenda (the Matthew
Arnold syndrome, that is, the culture of the players is conflated
with the culture of the analyst). In this section we are mainly
concerned with the first sense of inadequacy: oversimplification.

In its development in anthropology, at least, most of the inadequacies were artifacts of the evolution of the discipline and the
constraints of its dominant method, ethnography, as mentioned
earlier. Two basic problems sit at the center of these. First, from
both Tylor (who famously spoke of "that complex whole") and
Boas, and Boas's students (who emphasized, as well, holism and
the integration of traits and patterns), there was an assumption of
cultural coherence or overarching "systemicity." In its purest form
this was exemplified in Ruth Benedict's book—extremely influential in its time—*Patterns of Culture* (1934), where entire cultures (for example, Pueblo Zuni, Kwakiutl, Dobuan, and Plains
Indian) could be characterized by one powerful descriptor of their
dominant configuration (for example, Apollonian, Megalomaniac,
Paranoid, or Dionysian).[12] This coherence was overstated. It is
not the case, of course, that cultures lack any coherence or central
organizing tendencies whatsoever, but rather (to anticipate our
discussion) that (a) the extent of such overall coherence differs
from culture to culture (and from time to time); (b) coherence is
probably greatest in delimited cultural domains connected to specific social practices—that is, we should speak of coherences—
rather than in any overarching (cross-domain) way; and (c)
"coherence" does not preclude (interdomain) contradiction or paradox. In any event, the degree and nature of cultural coherence,
both within and across domains of social practice, are always

empirical questions. In fact, to anticipate our discussion once again, it is most probably during times of intense or deeply rooted social conflict that cultural coherence is most problematical.

The second basic problem concerned the locus of culture: Where did it stand? Specifically, was it located "inside" the individual (and thus connected to problems of psychology) or was it "outside," in superorganic structures above and beyond and external to individuals? Probably more ink has been spilled on this question than on any other in the social sciences. Boas's students split American anthropology in answering it one way or the other; British anthropologists, mostly following Emile Durkheim's lead, ignored the question by dismissing the relevance of psychology from first principles. Notice that Tylor answered the question in 1871 by saying, in effect, both. Culture was law, art, morals, and so on—things that are certainly *out there*, in books and courts, paintings and museums, sacred texts and windy cathedrals. These things were however "acquired by man" and therefore also, with respect to any individual, *in there*.[13] But even if we turned to the "out there" for culture's location, the question remained, Where? What sorts of structures or institutions contained culture? Tylor took "society" as his structure, and the Boasians implicitly followed suit. Perhaps this made sense in the relatively small-scale and face-to-face communities in which ethnographers traditionally worked. But this conceptualization resulted in a one-to-one mapping of culture and society ("Somali society is characterized by Somali culture") that either made them completely identical and interchangeable concepts or, as in Parsonian sociology, differentiated them as separate (sub)systems but retained a functionalist's bias for having them work together toward an overall systemic stability. In either case, the relationship between culture and society was presumed to be more or less transparent and unproblematical. But, in fact, problems are manifold: How many "Somali" (or Pueblo Zuni, Japanese, or American) societies and cultures are there? What sorts of social groups, structures, or institutions constitute a society? Can all of these come with their own cultures? Finally, the question we posed with regard to culture can be posed as easily with respect to society: Have we (sociologists, economists, political scientists, anthropologists) been overestimating its integration and coherence, its systemicity, all along?

From these two basic problems having to do with assumptions about the coherence and locus of culture, flow at least six mutually related ideas about culture that we call inadequate. These ideas are often found in the writings and practice of individuals, including those in conflict resolution who, borrowing an outmoded anthropological view of culture, seek to use a cultural approach in their work.[14]

1. *Culture is homogenous.* This presumes that a (local) culture is free of internal paradoxes and contradictions such that (a) it provides clear and unambiguous behavioral "instructions" to individuals—a program for how to act—or (b) once grasped or learned by an outsider, it can be characterized in relatively straightforward ways ("the Dobuans are paranoid"). A homogenous view of culture makes the second inadequate idea easier to sustain, namely that:

2. *Culture is a thing.* The reification of culture—regarding culture as a thing—leads to a notion that "it" is a thing that can act, almost independently of human actors. There is no hint of individual agency here. A good contemporary example of this sort of thinking is Samuel Huntington's "clash of civilizations" argument.[15] It is easy to fall into the semantic trap of reification. Read the earlier remark in this very essay about the constitutive power of culture to construct a definition of itself! The term is used as a shorthand way of referring, as we shall see, to bundles of complicated cognitive and perceptual *processes*, and it is a series of short (cognitive) steps from shorthand to metonymy to reification. But we should be on guard, particularly since by reifying culture it is easy to overlook intracultural diversity, underwriting the third inadequate idea:

3. *Culture is uniformly distributed among members of a group.* This idea imputes cognitive, affective, and behavioral uniformity to

all members of the group. Intracultural variation, whether at the individual or group level, is ignored or dismissed as "deviance." Connected to this is the further misconception that:

4. *An individual possesses but a single culture.* He or she is simply a Somali, a Mexican, or an American. Culture is thus synonymous with group identity. The root of this misconception stems from the privileging of what we can call tribal culture, ethnic culture, or national culture, over cultures that are connected, as we shall see, to very different sorts of groups, structures, or institutions. In part this came from the social settings in which anthropologists first developed the culture idea: small-scale and relatively socially undifferentiated tribal or ethnic groups. It was then compounded by political scientists who took up the notion of culture (as "political culture") and privileged the nation-state as their unit of analysis—hence the "national character" idea (to be discussed further in part II). In fact, as we will argue, for any individual, culture always comes in the plural. A person possesses and controls several cultures in the same way, as sociolinguists tell us, that even a so-called monolingual speaker controls different "registers" of the same language or dialect.[16]

5. *Culture is custom.* This idea holds that culture is structurally undifferentiated, that what you see is what you get. And mostly what you see (especially in a culture different from your own), naively of course, is custom. Culture here is virtually synonymous with "tradition," or customary ways of behaving. The important things to know, if you come from outside, are the customary rules for correct behavior. Culture here reduces to a sort of surface-level etiquette. Cultural variation is, as Peter Black once put it, merely a matter of "differential etiquette." Once again, individual agency is downplayed. In this view there is no sense of struggle, except perhaps for the struggle of deviants (see number 3, above) who cannot or will not abide by tradition and custom: after all, the smoothing out of difference and the mitigation of struggle are precisely what rules and etiquette are for.

15

6. *Culture is timeless.* Closely related to the culture-is-custom view (indeed, to all of the above views), the idea that culture is timeless imputes a changeless quality to culture, especially to so-called traditional ones. We speak here, for example, of "the Arab mind" as though a unitary cognizing element has come down to us from Muhammed's Mecca.

These six inadequate ideas about culture are related and mutually reinforcing. Using them, we argue, greatly diminishes the utility of the culture concept as an analytical tool for understanding social action, in this case, conflict and conflict resolution. But the whole issue of culture's analytical utility and of these inadequate ideas is complicated by the fact that *each one of these inadequate ideas is routinely invoked in what we have called the Matthew Arnold sense of culture.* This happens when culture is objectified by actors and used in politically charged—usually nationalistic, racialistic, or ethnic—discourses. Many of these discourses go way beyond the injuries inflicted by Arnold's snobbery, or even the class system of nineteenth-century England. As Rwanda, Burundi, Bosnia, and before them Nazi Germany all demonstrate, they are capable of provoking genocide. In fact, we have now identified one way in which one version of the culture concept, used as an ideological resource by contestants, is itself a source—or accelerant—of social conflict. One strategy for conflict resolution immediately presents itself: the proactive deconstruction, in the sense of debunking or unmasking, of these inadequate ideas. At least, this strategy logically falls out of seeing culture's role in the conflict. The enactment of such a strategy in places like Rwanda, Burundi, or Bosnia is, of course, another matter entirely.

Thinking about Culture

The point of listing bad ideas about culture is not just to criticize them but to help us to think more clearly about the concept. What all of the above inadequacies share is that they all simplify the idea of culture by making it seem more homogenous, stable, and superficial than the social and cognitive processes entailed by it. As it is, the concept of culture appears too soft or descriptive or unquantifiable for the methodological propensities of many positivistic social and behavioral scientists. In this case, what we propose will on first glance push it even further beyond the pale: we propose to complexify culture. We have already examined Tylor's foundational definition of the term. At the risk of adding yet another definition, we need to update Tylor's definition, as Theodore Schwartz has done:

> Culture consists of the derivatives of experience, more or less organized, learned or created by the individuals of a population, including those images or encodements and their interpretations (meanings) transmitted from past generations, from contemporaries, or formed by individuals themselves.[17]

The virtues of this definition are many. It conceptually connects culture to experience—to interpreted social action, to practice. It leaves the nature of culture's coherence (organization) an open question. It locates culture simultaneously "outside" individuals (in images or encodements or, as we prefer, schemas or models) and "inside." It addresses the structure and agency question by noting that individuals not only inherit and learn these images from the past and from contemporaries, but also are able to create new images themselves (some of which, presumably, are transmitted to others). Culture conceived in this way cannot, of course, be thought of as timeless or changeless. Thus this definition addresses some of the inadequacies noted above.

But two important qualifiers need to be added. First, the very general and diffuse formulation of "individuals in a population" must be sharpened sociologically. Individuals are organized in many potentially different ways in a population, by many different (and cross-cutting) criteria: for example, by kinship into families or clans; by language, race, or creed into ethnic groups; by socioeconomic characteristics into social classes; by geographical region into political interest groups; and by occupation or institutional memberships into unions, bureaucracies, industries, political parties, and militaries. The more complex and differentiated the social system, the more potential groups and institutions there are. And because each group or institution places individuals in different experiential worlds, and because culture derives in part from this experience, *each of these groups and institutions can be a potential container for culture*. Thus no population can be adequately characterized as a single culture or by a single cultural descriptor. As a corollary, the more complexly organized a population is on sociological grounds (class, region, ethnicity, and so on), the more complex will its cultural mappings appear. This is why the notion of "subculture(s)" is needed.[18]

The second qualification to this definition addresses the problem of assuming a uniform distribution of culture, that everyone shares the same cultural content (images and encodements) to the same degree. This assumption is unwarranted for two reasons, one sociogenic (having to do with social groups and institutions) and the other psychogenic (having to do with cognitive and affective processes characteristic of individuals). The first reason is a corollary of the social complexity issue noted above: Insofar as two individuals do not share the same sociological location in a given population (the same class, religious, regional, or ethnic backgrounds, for example), and insofar as these locations entail (sub)cultural differences, then the two individuals cannot share all cultural content perfectly. This is the sociogenic reason for the nonuniform distribution of culture. *Culture is socially distributed within a population.*

The second, psychogenic, reason culture is never perfectly shared by individuals in a population (no matter how, sociologically, the population is defined) has to do with the ways in which culture is to be found "in there," inside the individual. Here we are, broadly speaking, in the realm of psychodynamics, at least with respect to the ways and circumstances under which an individual receives or learns cultural images or encodements. Because of disciplinary boundaries and the epistemological blinders they often enforce, these sorts of generally psychological concerns are considered off-limits for many social scientists. For this reason, even many culture theorists have preferred to think of culture only as "out there," in public and social constructions, including symbols, that are wholly independent of mind—of cognition and affect.[19] Other scholars, especially from economics or international relations, as we shall see in the next section, prefer to ignore mind completely, treating it as essentially a "black box" phenomenon. But by ignoring mind they do not in fact escape broadly psychological issues; they merely end up relying on an unacknowledged, and fairly primitive, psychology.

It is by approaching mind—cognition and affect—that we can sort out the ways in which culture is causal, noting well our discussion, above, of the danger of reifying culture so that it simplemindedly causes conflict. It doesn't—it cannot. But cultural representations—images and encodements, schemas and models—are internalized by individuals. They are not internalized equally or all at the same level, however. Some are internalized very superficially and are the equivalent of cultural clichés. Others are deeply internalized and invested with emotion or affect. These can instigate behavior by being connected to desirable goals or end states. The more deeply internalized and affectively loaded, the more certain images or schemas are able to motivate action. This is the proper sense in which "culture is causal." It also accounts for the nonuniform distribution of culture, because for two individuals even the same cultural representation (resulting, for instance, from a completely shared sociological placement) can be differentially internalized.[20] This is the psychogenic reason for the nonuniform distribution of culture. *Culture is psychologically distributed within a population.* Of two revolutionaries, each sharing the same socioeconomic background and program, the same political ideology, and the same intellectual opposition to the regime in power, only one is motivated (by rage? by hatred? by childhood trauma? by what?) to throw the bomb. No one interested in social conflict or in conflict resolution can remain aloof from psychogenic—cognitive and affective—processes and their connections to social practice.

This is the final point that needs to be emphasized before moving on to conflict resolution proper: that culture, "the derivative of experience," is rooted deeply in ongoing or past social practice.[21] This means (contrary to the reified or stable or homogenous view of culture) that culture is to some extent always situational, flexible, and responsive to the exigencies of the worlds that individuals confront. This quality is also in the end what connects generic culture to local culture. Generically (evolutionarily) speaking, culture is adaptive, the primary way in which humans have adapted to their ever-changing environments. In this sense, too, culture has been described as "socially inherited solutions to life's problems (how to form families, obtain food and shelter, raise children, fight enemies, cure disease, control disputes, etc.)."[22] But locally speaking, in given situations these problems do not present themselves in exactly the same ways—the problems of subsistence are not the same for pastoral nomads and urban factory workers—and so we should expect that cultural solutions differ as well. They respond to requisite social practice; hence we have cultural variation and diversity.

It is important that adopting this problem-solving view of culture not commit us to the excessively optimistic presumptions of classical functionalism—that somehow the solutions found or used by a culture are always the right ones or the best ones. On the contrary, cultural solutions at the level of local knowledge and practice can be and very often have been (to use the locution of some colleagues) severely "suboptimal." Much of the field of conflict resolution, as we shall see in the next section, is based, in fact, on the fundamental belief that resort to physical violence in the processing of social conflict, up to and including war, is a prime example of wrongheaded problem solving. And the fact that most cultures at some point and in some circumstances sanction this solution is proof to these conflict resolutionists that culture needs to be not only analyzed and understood for purposes of activist conflict resolution, but rethought and re-imagined—*re-engineered*—as well. Thus, even as we turn now to consider conflict resolution theory and practice in the light of a more powerful analytical conception of culture, we cannot escape the other baggage the concept has always carried: the political.

Part II: Conflict Resolution

The essay's second part introduces two different conceptions of conflict resolution, broad and restricted, and carries the discussion of culture into the study of social conflict and conflict resolution, especially in the field of international relations. Paradoxically, international relations is a good place in which to examine culture, because the older, dominant paradigms of the discipline—realism and neorealism—have silenced or misappropriated cultural accounts in striking ways. All of the inadequate ideas about culture that were elucidated in part I can be found at work when, as in "national character" studies, international relations, retaining the state as its foundational concept, has tried to grapple with culture. In newer, cognitivist approaches to the field, however, there have been openings toward an understanding of culture very close to the one we have proposed. Within international relations, we focus particularly on negotiation as an area in which cultural accounts, despite the reservations of skeptics such as I. W. Zartman, have made some headway. Indeed, we use the skeptics' critiques to explore the idea of a culture of diplomacy, which illustrates what we mean by expanding the relevance of cultural analyses beyond such collectivities as tribe or ethnic group. Finally, responding to the realists once again, we consider the very thorny problem of power and culture.

23

Thinking about Social Conflict—and "Resolution"

Conflict is a feature of all human societies and, potentially, an aspect of all social relationships. How we conceptualize the root causes of conflict will determine to a large degree the sorts of conflict resolution theories and practices we favor, or even think possible. Likewise, how we conceive of conflict's causes will determine the importance of culture in our theories and practices of conflict resolution. Here are two widely cited definitions that highlight different root causes of conflict:

> Conflict. . . . A struggle over values and claims to scarce status, power, and resources, a struggle in which the aims of opponents are to neutralize, injure, or eliminate rivals.[23]
>
> Conflict means perceived divergence of interest, or a belief that parties' current aspirations cannot be achieved simultaneously.[24]

Although the first definition, Lewis Coser's, is more comprehensive (in allowing both "values" and the qualifying "claims to" to modify the main clause), it focuses on the idea of scarcity as the cause of conflict. (It also pays attention to conflict's consequences: "struggle" strongly implies violence.) The second definition emphasizes perception and belief. Broadly speaking, these two definitions suggest two major approaches to conflict and, thus to conflict resolution. The first definition underlines scarcity of material (among other) resources, and power. The second highlights perception and belief, and by extension, differing interpretations of these. The first seems to move parties rather directly to contention, to struggle. The second seems to invite the possibilities of talk, of negotiation.

Conflict resolution looks rather different depending on which sense of conflict we begin with. If we combine the definitions and moreover emphasize the connectedness of the two parties, we can say that conflict occurs when two related parties—individuals, groups, communities, or nation-states—find themselves divided by perceived incompatible interests or goals or in

competition for control of scarce resources.[25] This hybrid definition of conflict immediately suggests three strategies for conflict
resolution. First, if conflict is an attribute of the social relationship between the parties, then one or both of the parties can
sever (or "exit") the relationship and end the conflict. Second, if
the conflict arises from the parties' perceptions or beliefs that
they are incompatible or that resources are scarce (since parties
act on the basis of perception and belief), then if it can be dem-
onstrated that the perceptions or beliefs are false (for example,
that the parties really do share interests and goals but for some
reason cannot see this or that the resources are not really scarce
but are, or can be made to be, plentiful), then the correction of
misperception can end the conflict. Finally, because not all social
relationships are easily severed, and not all perceptions of incom-
patibility or scarcity are demonstrably wrong, the parties can move
to resolve their conflict by engaging in the kind of contention
that Coser describes: a struggle wherein one party seeks to dominate (or eradicate) the other and thereby control scarce resources.

One question that arises immediately about these three strategies is whether they are all manifestations of "conflict resolution." Is a party's avoidance of conflict by the strategy of severing
its relationship with the other party or, in yielding completely to
the other party's claims, by "lumping it" (putting up with it), the
same sort of resolution as negotiating an agreement in which,
say, resources are shared? War is perhaps Coser's idea of struggle
carried to its extreme. Is war also conflict resolution? Some of the
conceptual problems we encountered in defining culture are to
be found as well in defining conflict resolution. And some of the
apparent confusion in the emergent field of conflict resolution—
theorists and practitioners speaking past one another or engaging in polemic—is the result of these different base-line
conceptions of what resolution means.

There are, broadly speaking, two conceptions of conflict resolution. The first is general and refers to *any strategy that brings a
socially visible or public episode of conflict (a dispute) to an end.* Under

this conception, all of the following count as modes of conflict resolution: exit or lumping it (both forms of one party's retreat from the conflict); negotiations to share resources or adjust perceptions; intervention by an authoritative third party who stipulates a solution; and struggle up to and including the elimination of one party as a viable contestant.

The second conception of conflict resolution, the one that has arisen with the formal emergence of the field or quasi discipline of conflict resolution, is defined much more narrowly and precisely to exclude retreat (even if voluntary), coercion, and, therefore, war as modes of conflict resolution. Some theorists of the "new" conflict resolution even want to exclude negotiation that aims at simple divisions of resources—to exclude bargaining toward a compromise—as a mode of "genuine" conflict resolution. Genuine resolution is differentiated from conflict "management" or conflict "regulation," from dispute "settlement" or conflict "mitigation."[26] Each of these may well have a role to play—by, for example, dampening or halting violence—but they should not be mistaken for *resolution*. Resolution aims somehow to get to the root causes of a conflict and not merely to treat its episodic or symptomatic manifestation, that is, a particular dispute. In this way conflict resolution shows its affinity to peace studies rather than, say, to strategic security studies, where we can find the first sense of resolution predominant.[27] In fact, the restricted sense of resolution owes much to the seminal distinction that Johan Galtung made between "negative peace" (defined simply as the absence of war) and "positive peace" (defined as a societal condition in which structures of domination and exploitation, which underlie war, have been eliminated).[28]

In conflict resolution theory this Galtungian sense of resolution has been advocated most forcefully by two theorists who in other ways, and particularly with respect to the role of culture in conflict resolution, disagree on the essential nature of the enterprise. One is John Burton, who invented the expression "conflict *provention*" to refer to a kind of resolution that seeks to eliminate the root causes of the conflict or, as he has put it, to seek the "solution of the problems which led to the conflictual behavior in the first place."[29] The other is John Paul Lederach, who, believing that conflict resolution as a term already has too much "management" and "settlement" semantic baggage associated with it (on the problem of baggage, pace culture!), wants to abandon the term in favor of "conflict transformation."[30]

The sorts of conflict resolution practices or techniques prescribed by these "restricted resolution" theorists will be discussed in a later section. But we have already mentioned that Burton and Lederach, sharing a restricted sense of resolution, nevertheless differ profoundly on the role of culture in attaining it. Let us then return to culture, by way of the two conceptions of conflict that we began with: the one centered on scarcity and power, the other on perception and belief.

Realism and the Absence of Culture in International Relations Theory

On the one hand, it is apparent that the idea of culture we have proposed will especially resonate with those who understand conflict as a matter of perception and belief, of cognition and affect. On the other hand, those who see conflict as essentially a matter of competition by parties over scarce resources or (material) interests will be less appreciative of the usefulness of the culture concept, particularly *to the extent that they also exclude perception and belief as having any significant effects on the parties' respective calculations of scarcity, power, or interests.* Such an exclusion would make sense for one or both of the following reasons: (a) a view of the world such that notions of scarcity, resources, and interests seem self-evident and unchanging—simply out there for everyone to see and agree on; and (b) a conception of relevant *actors* in the world that erases any possibilities for conceiving difference, in favor of conceiving similarities. Taken together, both of these conditions neatly describe the so-called realist paradigm that dominated international relations theory after World War II (and has hardly disappeared).

Culture—local culture, to be exact—focuses our attention on differences among social groups or societies, on diversity. In the field of international relations, with its concern with *states* as the unit-actor of action and analysis, societies—each one a potentially complex entity—are already reduced to the shorthand of states. The realist paradigm sees the international system in terms of internally undifferentiated, monolithic states, each acting according to a rational calculus in order to maximize security (among other utilities) by marshaling and projecting power to coerce adversaries and co-opt allies.[31] The state system is a balance-of-power system, set within an environment of presumed incipient chaos and disorder.[32]

Any one of the major assumptions of realist thinking can render culture invisible. First, the assumption of undifferentiated states suppresses any possible differences among them, or at least renders differences essentially monodimensional: states need be distinguished from one another only by their relative (that is, susceptible to an ordinal ranking) possession of power. Second, the assumption of rationality in the behavior of states suppresses consideration of other modes of reasoning or decision-making imperatives. Third, the assumption (linked to rationality) of maximizing utilities (for instance, of security) imposes on all the actors in the system a single, universalizing standard of measurement.[33] Finally, all this suppression of difference in favor of sameness is possible because the strong force holding the chaotic system of states together is power. Power is the ultimate good and the fundamental resource: it is *the* reality that drives realism. The state system is conceived to conform to the "laws" of this reality. The concept of "interest" is defined in terms of power; indeed, all politics is defined in terms of power. The following is from the sixth edition of Hans Morgenthau's classic, *Politics among Nations:*

All politics, domestic and international, reveals three basic patterns; that is, all political phenomena can be reduced to one of three basic types. A political polity seeks either to keep power, to increase power, or to demonstrate power.[34]

Perhaps much of the above should be placed now in the past tense, because realism and balance-of-power thinking are no longer prevalent. Realism always had its philosophical counterpart in international relations, a position faintly praised (and so damned) as "idealism." This view stressed beliefs, values, ideologies, and ideas as motors of international affairs. At first glance, idealism is more sympathetic and amenable than realism is to a cultural perspective. After all, a concern with culture is itself historically linked to idealist and "mentalist"—*subjectivist*—concerns. And the concept of culture we presented earlier does use the notion of ideational codes of one sort or another. But there is a difference between our concept of culture, which is grounded in practice and social action *in* the world, and classical idealism. Much of the idealist perspective reduces to a mentalism that is itself universalized, based on, for example, presumptions about natural law and its own version of a univariate human nature. In its liberal, utopian guise, idealism replaces the realists' will to dominate with the will to cooperate.[35] Once again, the effect is to eradicate differences in favor of sameness—and culture is about difference. In its pessimistic, Spenglerian guise, idealism may even adopt realism's power politics to create the "clash of civilizations" drama. Here the effect is to suppress the heterogeneity and complexities of culture in favor of spurious homogeneity and unexplained (social) action at a distance. Often, the hidden assumption is that the mere existence of cultural difference (conceived as values, ideologies, beliefs) is sufficient to cause conflict. This view makes "culture" into a cause of conflict. On the whole, it is a specious view, one that confuses deeply rooted and constitutive *cultural* difference with socially constructed and politically motivated *ethnic* difference. In the simplest sense of a cultural misunderstanding, a "failure to communicate" is essentially a translation problem that is easily diagnosed and fixed. In the sense that journalists or ideologues speak of *kulturkampf*, "culture" is a label in a struggle about something quite different, such as resources or power. The mere existence of cultural differences is rarely a cause of conflict. This hardly diminishes culture's importance to conflict analysis or resolution, however, because it is *always* the lens through which the causes of conflict are refracted.

Perhaps more than anything else, it has been the collapse of the Soviet Union as the other world superpower, and the end of the Cold War alignments of the superpowers with their allied or client states, that have challenged some of the tenets of realist thinking. It is not just that states are breaking up into smaller states. At the very beginning of the post–Cold War era, James Rosenau wrote with great prescience of a new bifurcation of world politics between what he called a "sovereignty-bound world" and a "sovereignty-free" one.[36] What *are* states—or an international relations theory of them—absent sovereignty? Certainly, after the breakup of the Soviet Union, after Chechnya, Yugoslavia, Somalia, Liberia, Afghanistan, or Albania, after such notions as fragile states, collapsed states, or imagined states have entered our consciousness, it is more difficult to conceive of states in their hard-shelled Westphalian form. We have a harder time now not looking inside them, partly because many have self-disemboweled. It is harder, too, to see them as monolithic, or as speaking authoritatively with one (regime or governmental) voice in the name of their citizens. (Think even of democratic states in Europe or North America: of Quebecois separatism or the brittleness of Flemish-Walloon ties in Belgium.) States can now be seen as (often unstable) tropes, metonyms for competing congeries of internal ethnic, nationalist, regional, religious, racial, or class interest. Domestic politics affects international politics (nowadays a truism). More often than not, domestic politics thoroughly undermines pretensions of state-level rationality or utility-maximizing behaviors. *Here* we are closer to culture than we were with idealism. For here we are dealing with identity politics and nationalist discourses, with suicidal irredentisms and genocidal ethnic cleansings: with operationalized primordialisms that have little to do with rational decision making or problem solving. With genocide we are no longer in the land of cost-benefit analyses; we are instead in the murderous realm of the senses.

Political Culture and National Character

Realism as the dominant paradigm in international relations theory suppressed the idea of culture but did not completely erase it. There were always political scientists and scholars of international relations who used the idea of culture. Certainly, the names Gabriel Almond, Sidney Verba, and Lucian Pye, among others especially associated with comparative or development-oriented research, have been associated with the idea of political culture since the late 1950s. Stressing the subjectivist orientation of political actors, or such notions as values, these scholars were usually lumped into the idealists' camp.[37] As noted earlier, the idea of political culture was the political scientist's way of sharpening the omnibus sense of culture (that complex whole) bequeathed to anthropology from Tylor's day. It made sense if one focused on politics—and wanted a slightly more nuanced understanding of it than realism's power! power! power!—to restrict culture to those beliefs or attitudes having to do with the domain of politics, governance, or authority; though from an anthropologist's perspective this narrowing has always seemed restrictive: for politics is surely constituted out of a total cultural matrix, rather than the reverse. Nevertheless, the main problem with the political culture idea has not been so much the restricted range of its relevance (this is perhaps defensible on heuristic grounds) as it has been the inadequacy of the concept of culture that has been employed.

We are back to the six inadequate ideas of culture discussed earlier. Taken together, these six ideas make up a notion of culture that looks a lot like the concept that motivated the national character studies within anthropology of the 1940s and 1950s. This research tradition has long been discredited and surpassed within anthropology itself, but it went on to (mis)represent *the*

31

anthropological idea of culture to several generations of political scientists. And because developments in one discipline are only recognized in related disciplines after a time lag, it influenced the development in the 1960s of "political culture" within political science. (Culture *as* national character is an idea also found in related studies of international and intercultural conflict resolution, as we shall see.) In the sixth edition of Morgenthau's text we read of national character as

> the fact—contested but (it seems to us) incontestable, *especially in view of the anthropological concept of the "culture pattern"*—that certain qualities of intellect and character occur more frequently and are more highly valued in one nation than in another.[38] (Emphasis added.)

Referring to this essentially atavistic usage of culture in political science and international relations, Robert A. Rubinstein focused precisely on the need to replace the static "culture as patterns" view of things (the title of Ruth Benedict's *1934* book, after all), with the dynamic "culture as process" view.[39] "Process" itself may be too mild a word to communicate the often heated dynamics that swirl around parties' contested versions of national cultures (rather than characters), as elites and other contestants struggle to impose their own conception of nation and peoplehood as the dominant one.[40] Then too, for Morgenthau national character was primarily important because (along with something he called "national morale") it fed directly into national power. Thus he paints us such pithy portraits as "the elementary force and persistence of the Russians, the individual initiative and inventiveness of the Americans, the undogmatic common sense of the British, the discipline and thoroughness of the Germans."[41]

Consider those terse national characterizations. (Consider also that they remained in the 1985 edition of the book.) In some ways the national character view of culture—culture as stable, homogenous, customary, reified, and singular—fit very well the needs of realist theorists in international relations, paradoxically, even when it was ignored by them. It fit realist theory because such a view of culture allowed the unproblematic shorthanding, or the congruent mapping, of *state*, *society*, and *culture* to take place. (Only fairly recently have "state-society" relations become problematized within the field of international relations.) The national character view of culture was mostly ignored, however, because, as noted, realist theory assumed that the state was the only actor of consequence and that it behaved rationally to maximize utilities. In the end, too, culture had to be ignored since even the most mechanical of national character studies hinted at the possibility, at least, of other rationalities and other perceptions of the public good. As an epitome (decidedly *not* a mechanical one), go back to Ruth Benedict's subversive classic *The Chrysanthemum and the Sword*.[42] Among other things, Benedict's work demonstrates that when culture, even in its deficient national character manifestation, was taken seriously in the formulation of foreign policy (here, wartime policy), the results could be powerful—and fortuitous. Michael Vlahos, for example, who served as the director of the State Department's Center for the Study of Foreign Affairs, has written that Benedict's wartime work and analysis—her book—"is credited with sparing Kyoto from the Bomb. . . . [S]he argued that dropping U-235 on Kyoto would destroy Japan's very soul."[43]

The conspicuous absence of culture in realist international relations theorizing is multidetermined. One reason lies with the deficiencies of an outmoded (though still used) culture concept. We have argued here that the culture concept could be ignored because, in its inadequate form, it stressed patterning, stability, singularity, and homogeneity. It certainly did not feature a concern with struggle, change, and power—qualities to be found in abundance in the world.[44] By contrast, realist international relations theory has faced power from the beginning. But what it has lacked is the slightest suspicion that the wielders of power—that is, states—might not all be cut from the same cloth. Or that assumptions of state-level rationality are overdrawn. Or, more radically, that even power is not the straightforward or self-evident entity that Morgenthau, E. H. Carr, or Kenneth Waltz presumes it to be. In other words, realist international relations theory had its own assumptions of stability, singularity, and homogeneity to contend with. And these are *hidden* assumptions—which brings us to the second reason for culture's absence in realist international relations theorizing.

Realism, with its positivistic epistemology, claims to present accurate and veridical descriptions of the world out there (the international state system) "as it really is." But a growing critique from within international relations proposes something very different: that realism is actually constructing a vision of that world as realist thinkers, in their hearts and minds, *know* it has to be.[45] The implications for conflict resolution theories and practices that derive from realism's construction of such a world—and those from reactions against it—are to be considered in subsequent sections. The implications for the concept of culture are rather different: they imply that realism itself is a cultural construction, perhaps even a post–World War II reaction to the perceived failures in the interwar years of an American (and, more generally, a democratic Western European) foreign policy based on Wilsonian idealism.[46] Vlahos makes a similar point on a smaller canvas, just after noting how Benedict's insights into Japanese culture—and her successful communication of them to relevant American political/military actors—saved Kyoto from the Bomb. He opined that the brief postwar interest in culture in the U.S. foreign policy establishment ultimately floundered because the main message of culture—difference and diversity—was part of "an American intellectual movement that could not, in the end, transcend the American spirit of the age: the mission to export American culture everywhere."[47] In other words, aspects of postwar American culture foreclosed the foreign policy establishment's intellectual acceptance of the analytical utility of the concept of *culture*. *Culture was blinded by itself to itself*. It is hard here to resist committing the sin of reification, and hard, too, not to acknowledge once again the real difficulties of the term "culture" and why Raymond

Williams called it one of the most complicated words in the English language.

Culture in International Relations Theory: Cognitivist Approaches

Earlier we noted that conflict has been understood from one of two broad perspectives. One emphasizes scarcity and material interests, the other cognition, perception, and belief. The realist paradigm is based on the first orientation, with the added presumption of state-level rationality. The concept of culture as we developed it, however, is rooted more closely to the second orientation, stressing cognitivist notions like image, schema, and ideational encodements. It is not surprising therefore that theories of international relations and conflict that focus on material concerns will be less sympathetic to the uses of culture than will cognitivist theories of international relations or conflict. Cognitivist theories all argue for the social constructedness of world politics and conflict. Not all constructionist theories are cognitivist, of course: some Marxist, feminist, or postmodern theorists are suspicious of cognitivist claims as part of a general hostility toward what they call "psychologizing" sociopolitical phenomena.[48] But all constructionists agree that "the fundamental structures of international politics are social rather than strictly material (a claim that opposes materialism) and that these structures shape actors' identities and interests, rather than just their behavior (a claim that opposes rationalism)."[49] Not surprisingly, it is researchers in the constructionist orientation in international relations and conflict studies, and especially the cognitivists among them, who are potentially the most sympathetic to cultural approaches.

One of the pioneers here is Robert Jervis, who twenty years ago argued that international politics was often driven by actor-centered cognitive processes involving systematic mutual misperceptions of, among other things, other actors' motives, intentions, autonomy, and degree of rationality.[50] Interestingly, Jervis quite explicitly left out of his work any consideration of compounding problems of cultural differences and actors' perceptions, because he knew that such differences would have the effect of magnifying perceptual distortions. He wanted to make his strong case for the influence of cognitive factors in situations where actors shared a common culture. Nowadays, of course, we would even make such assumptions of totally shared common culture the subject of empirical inquiry.[51]

We might say that Jervis pioneered a cognitivist view of international relations in that he asserted not the ironclad and crisply inflexible cost-benefit logic of the state system—what we encounter in Morgenthau and other realists—but rather, as we might put it today, the *fuzzy logic* of all the actors in it.[52] The idea of fuzzy logic is important to keep in mind. When we think of culture as socially transmitted or learned solutions to life's problems, we should not let the problem-solving sense of culture lure us into thinking of it as providing a kind of logic as understood by Aristotle or even logicians from early in the twentieth century. Insofar as culture prescribes for individuals "a logic," we would do well to think of it not in terms of the crisp distinctions of traditional logic, where statements are "true" or "false," but rather in terms of the more rubbery statements of so-called fuzzy logic. Fuzzy logic deals with propositions that are more or less true or false. It deals with graded membership in nonstable classes or sets. It is a logic for dealing with uncertainties. This is a much better way for thinking about the relationship between culture and cognition, or of culture as the way we solve problems and reason our way through the world, if only because the world regularly presents us with new problems to solve, with propositions that are not unambiguously true or false—with uncertainty.[53]

Thinking in terms of logic, even fuzzy logic, orients us around the notion of "proposition," and from there it is a small step to thinking of cognition (or culture) in propositional terms, for example, as systems of rules or, more colloquially, even of recipes for behavior. There are other terms—ones we have mentioned, such as "image" or "schema"—that free us from the bounds of linear-leaning rules toward more visual metaphors for cognition and culture, ones that move us to thinking of cognition not solely as serial or linear processes but as associative, networked, or parallel-processing activities.[54] Schemas are networked cognitive structures that contain "canned" procedures or instructions for dealing with recurrent situations or for assimilating new situations into recurrent ones. Metaphor is another idea that scholars in anthropology, international relations, or conflict studies have begun to use to get at complex cognitive and social phenomena.[55] The radicalness of this shift, especially for international relations, cannot be overstated. For example, in realist international relations theory, "security" is taken unselfconsciously to be a utility that states seek rationally to maximize; like almost everything else, it is defined by reference to power. Cognitivists will reverse figure and ground: *security* becomes a metaphor to be unpacked and deconstructed, opened up in order to examine the assumptions, presuppositions, *as schemas, plans, or scripts for action*, that are contained within it. This, at least, is what Paul Chilton did so masterfully with the Cold War notion of "security."[56]

An interest in metaphor was part of a larger turn in the social sciences away from positivism (and for some, away from causal or functional explanation) toward interpretation and a Weberian-inflected emphasis on meaning and understanding. The main thrust consisted of revising the traditional, Aristotelian view of metaphor as something limited to poetics or rhetoric, something peripheral to the main tasks of language and communication—merely figures of speech that embellish or adorn. Now, metaphor is seen as something central to cognition, including reasoning and memory.[57] It is also seen as constitutive of culture.[58] This is important, since it is at the level of culture that we can think of metaphor as transcending the cognition of any one individual. It is also how we can link metaphor as a purely cognitive phenomenon to something that is connected with actors' interactions with one another, and to what linguists, referring to the action and communicational contexts of language, call *pragmatics*.

There is another conceptual connection between metaphor and culture: both derive from individuals' experiences—and then shape *subsequent* experience. Like Lakoff and Johnson, many early analysts of metaphor stressed what they called the universal aspects of metaphor, those arising from universal aspects of (a mostly physical) environment: for example, directionality (UP or DOWN, INSIDE or OUTSIDE); motion; or, critically, the universal topography of the human body. We might argue that these constitute core metaphors. But environments differ, and not all human experience is universal. If this is the case, then we would expect metaphors to differ from experiential world to experiential world, from culture to culture.

We would also expect metaphors or, more precisely, what Oscar Nudler called "metaphor dialogue," to be especially mportant in *inter*cultural encounters.[59] This is because, viewed functionally, the main task of a metaphor is to map what is known about one domain onto a less well-known domain.[60] Put differently, metaphor is another way we deal with uncertainty. Intercultural encounters often bring the known (say, oneself) into contact with the less known (the other), and they often involve uncertainty. If metaphors were always shared, then intercultural encounters could be metaphor dialogues in the fullest sense of the term. But crossing cultural boundaries may also involve crossing metaphor boundaries. And, as often happens when we cross from one language community to another, that is the point where dialogue becomes problematical. When we speak about the perceptual or cognitive aspects of social conflict, we are perforce speaking about understanding the parties' schemas and metaphors. When we speak about the perceptual or cognitive aspects of conflict resolution, in *practice* this means (as we shall see below) trying to transform the relevant schemas and metaphors.

Here we return to the (linguistic) pragmatic and communicational entailments of metaphor, schema, perception, and culture. In both international relations theorizing and the actual conduct of international affairs—and for conflict resolution theory and practice—this ultimately means coming to grips with that most ubiquitous of human interactional activities,[61] and the most fundamental form of conflict resolution: *negotiation*. We turn to this now.

Culture and Negotiation

Negotiation has been defined in many ways, but most speak of negotiation as a process of communication between at least two parties, from individuals to states (in which case it goes by a special name, diplomacy).[62] In negotiation, the two parties become interlocutors: they engage in an extended conversation about their dispute. They exchange information relating to their positions and perhaps (though not always explicitly) to the interests that underlie those positions.[63] They try to educate one another.[64] They may also try to persuade one another, in which case the conversation can become mutually rhetorical or accusatory.[65] (And often the parties end up, as they say, "talking past one another.") Finally, they may even try to coerce one another. In this case we may say that they have fallen back to a different form of conflict behavior entirely, for how can one discuss and coerce at the same time?[66]

This last point, and even the possibility of a coercive diplomacy, should remind us that although negotiation is the most fundamental form of conflict management or settlement or even resolution, it is only contingently related to these outcomes. Both parties may wish to end or mitigate their dispute. In that case, the aim of negotiation is to use the medium of discussion to try to resolve their divergence of interest. But negotiation could be another sort of tool in a conflict situation. One or both parties may wish to enter negotiations for public relations or public opinion purposes. Or one party may use negotiations as a stalling tactic to give it time to marshal its forces for attack or defense. Sir Harold Nicolson may have defined diplomacy wholly in terms of negotiation, and negotiation in terms of gentlemanly principles such as "moderation and fair-dealing"; but using negotiation as a stalling tactic reminds us that there are other possible aims to negotiation and therefore other ways to parse diplomacy. Take, for example, Wynn Catlin's definition: "Diplomacy is the art of saying 'Nice doggie' till you can find a rock."[67]

Nevertheless, whatever its uses, negotiation is *about* communicating, and even at the state level, communication implies the existence of situated actors. We say "situated" because the closer one gets to actual negotiations and real interlocutors, the more difficult it becomes to theorize even interstate negotiations as reducible to rational, utilities-maximizing decision making, where decision making can itself be reduced to an autistic, hermetically sealed, "black box" process. And one way in which actors are situated is by culture(s). Perhaps this is why the one area of international relations theorizing, even under the realist's sway, that has appeared relatively open to the admission of cultural perspectives has been that concerned with international negotiations.[68] For example, Hopmann, as part of an exhaustive study of the U.S.-Soviet 1962–63 Test Ban Negotiations, writes:

> I cannot overemphasize the importance of clear and effective communication to the success of international negotiations. All negotiations depend on communication, and this is one area in which the human element cannot be discounted. Such effective communication, especially across national, cultural, and linguistic boundaries, requires constant attention to make sure that messages are sent clearly and interpreted similarly by both parties. It also requires an awareness of the individual and group sources of potential misinterpretation so that conscious efforts must be made in negotiations to communicate in spite of these differences.[69]

Culture has worked its way into the international negotiations literature for two reasons. First, because negotiation is about communication, and a focus on communication makes it difficult to avoid seeing the "human element": subjectivity, cognition, and context—culture. Second, this is an area of international relations scholarship where the active (or more often, perhaps, retired) *practitioner* has something to contribute; the players have something to say. Practitioners—presidents, ministers, or diplomats—who have negotiated with foreign interlocutors often have an intuition that culture matters in ways that abstracted game-theorists usually succeed in ignoring. These insights are typically recounted in their memoirs; it is hard to read the various memoirs of a Kissinger, Carter, or Nixon (just to stick with Americans) and not come upon nuggets of national character wisdom about dealing with the Italians, Chinese, Arabs and Israelis, or Russians. Sometimes, when memoir merges with hornbook, we get a pellucid look into the national character of the diplomat—or, more precisely in our terms, into the dominant schema, for instance the *commercial transaction*—that structures that actor's diplomatic and negotiation domain. Thus, for example, our exemplary Sir Harold Nicolson:

> [T]he art of negotiation is essentially a mercantile art, and . . .
> the success of British diplomacy is . . . founded on the sound
> business principles of moderation, fair-dealing, reasonableness,
> credit, compromise, and a distrust of all surprises or sensational
> extremes. . . . [T]he foundation of good diplomacy is the same as
> the foundation of good business.[70]

But the more interesting and useful work of this sort is that done by practitioners who have tried to minimize the grosser national character aspects, factor out moralizing prescriptiveness, and systematize their insights with more coherent linkages to relevant regional history or to social science theory.[71] And finally, some specialists in international relations, not themselves practitioners or professional diplomats, have also taken up this area.[72] The ways in which these latter writers have tried more systematically to conceptualize culture is something we will take up in a later section. But it is important now to consider the views of some culture skeptics, those who argue that culture has a relatively small impact on international negotiations or conflict resolution. We will start with negotiations and the views of William Zartman; later, with regard to conflict resolution (narrowly defined), the views of John Burton will be considered.

Culture and International Negotiation: Some Skeptics

"Culture is indeed relevant to the understanding of the negotiation process," Zartman writes, adding tartly, "every bit as relevant as [the] breakfast [the negotiators ate], and to much the same extent."[73] In part, Zartman dismisses culture for methodological reasons: the concept seems insufficiently operationalizable—tautological—and too vague for linear univariate causal models predictive of behavior. To this we must agree but, along with Faure and Rubin, also add that Zartman has "confused tautology with complexity and dynamism," failing to see that part of this complex dynamism means that culture is always tautological: both dependent and independent variable, "product and source," of social action (including negotiations).[74] Elsewhere, however, Zartman has proposed other reasons why culture is in effect peripheral to negotiation; and these are worth looking at in greater detail.

The first reason holds that negotiation is, at some deep structural level, "a universal process, using a finite number of behavioral patterns, and that cultural differences are simply differences in style and language." The second reason is, as we shall see, slightly subversive of the first. It holds that culture doesn't matter: "By now the world has established an international diplomatic culture that soon socializes its members into similar behavior. Even the Chinese [!] have learned to play the U.N. game by its rules."[75] There is also a third argument that Zartman does not explicitly offer but which is potentially an important one. This argument, a precipitate of realism, holds that whatever the status of culture—structurally deep or superficial, generic or local—it doesn't matter, because culture is inevitably trumped by power. Let us take each argument in turn.

Negotiation is universal. At once this takes us into the marked tension between conceptions of generic and local culture(s), and all the freighted arguments about universal human nature. One response is to enlarge our conception of negotiation beyond the simplest sense of what communicating means—to explore Hopmann's warning, cited earlier, in greater depth. And we shall. But let us for the moment accept Zartman's analogy with style and language and even grant his assertion that a finite number of behavioral patterns make up negotiation. Even granting this universalistic position, international negotiators still face the pragmatic, if humbler, issue of how much interference or inefficiency is introduced to negotiations if inadequate attention to culture is paid. In the discourse of the realists, what are the costs? Think about the language analogy: It is one thing to argue that, say, English and Arabic are, at the deepest structural levels of neurological functioning the same linguistic or cognitive entity. It is another to underestimate their impressive differences or to expect that translations can be done by anyone or that, once done by even a bilingual speaker, they are unproblematically transparent. On the contrary, even a minimal exposure to a multicultural, polyglot world convinces most of us that problems of translation are be taken very seriously indeed. Moreover—to return to the language analogy momentarily—reducing the *production* of language to a finite number of *behavioral* patterns—for example, air must pass through a vocal apparatus such that vocal cords must vibrate—tells us very little about interlocutory language-in-use (the other sense of pragmatics), about meaning and understanding. In light of this, a more recent dismissal of culture by Zartman, also by analogy, is quite revealing. "Culture is to negotiation," he writes, "what birds flying into engines are to flying airplanes or, at most, what weather is to aerodynamics—practical impediments."[76] Yes, they are, but one also shudders at the consequences of birds in turbines or sudden wind shear: crashes and catastrophe and death. What are the consequences of international negotiations that "crash" along analogous lines? In some cases, they are also catastrophe and death.

Diplomacy is universal. Zartman's second argument about why culture is as consequential as breakfast is that there now exists a universal, worldwide culture of diplomacy (*even* the Chinese have got it): in effect, at least in the diplomatic world, we all now speak the same language in the same style. There are several responses to this, but let us begin with the one that takes note of how this assertion subverts Zartman's larger claim that culture doesn't matter. For what Zartman here argues for is the power of culture—the *culture of diplomacy*. Of course, Zartman may never have been speaking against culture to begin with, but perhaps only against the relevance of something called "national culture"—the latter-day residue of national character—as an explanatory variable. In fact, some of Zartman's criticism of culture is directed toward the inadequate conceptions of it that we have explored. There are indeed limitations to making the structural level of national culture our main one, even if it has the advantage of providing us with handy labels—Mexican, Japanese, Somali, and so on. Culture is not monolithic and restricted in its effects to a single level of social structure, including the nation-state; culture does not map transparently onto something called nationality. And "it" never determines individual behavior in a monocausal way. Individuals, as we said, are carriers of multiple cultures.

If we focus on culture as connected to social practice, as derivative of actors' experience in and of their worlds, then the concept gains in significance when we see that it is a way of organizing our thinking about the great varieties of social practice and their corresponding social institutions and structures. So, of course, it makes sense to speak of the "culture of professions" or occupations, or the culture of institutions, in addition to the culture of more traditional social entities like tribe, clan, or cult. Any given individual is in fact likely to be enculturated into a number of different worlds as he or she is socialized into a number of different groups or institutions. What perhaps most sharply characterizes individuals in the condition we sometimes call modernity are the sheer number and the emphatic compulsoriness of some institutions or structures to which individuals are socialized—and the sometimes intersecting, self-contradictory cultural worlds they might inhabit.[77]

Indeed, this is precisely what makes contemporary international negotiations so complex: they are multicultural arenas in which national culture is but one component and not always the crucial one. Referring to one such negotiation, Hopmann writes:

> It is not surprising that in negotiations such as the Strategic Arms Reduction talks (START) between the United States and the former Soviet Union, some of the most productive meetings took place across the table between expert groups of military officers or even intelligence officers of the two countries. . . . Although cultural differences did not wash out completely, they were often overwhelmed by the professional interest and curiosity [and *culture!*—K.A.] that the groups of professional advisors from the two countries held in common with one another and did not share with some other delegates from their own countries.[78]

To return to Zartman, there is no denying the existence of a diplomatic culture. It has certainly been around long enough, and its values, norms, and practices have been formed and upheld by some fairly powerful state and imperial entities since the eighteenth century or so.[79] There are academies and training programs for aspiring diplomats throughout North America and Europe, and there is the venerable and irreplaceable practice of mentoring and apprenticeship in ministries and embassies, where, through practice, one learns this culture. It is, as Glen Fisher points out, a culture "largely based on Western practices and even on the English language, so many otherwise 'foreign' counterparts are accommodating to the American style of negotiating."[80] Thus it is also not surprising that we find programs that explicitly train or socialize so-called Third World diplomats to function in the Western-inflected world arena. The Austrian career diplomat Winfried Lang describes a handbook "addressed to Third World negotiators" as providing "ample advice on how to negotiate with counterparts from the United States and Japan, on how to react most efficiently to the negotiating styles of these two major *donor* nations" (emphasis added).[81] The "donor" part is emphasized because it reflects the homely homily about how those who pay the piper get to call the tunes: we can probably wait a long time for the International Monetary Fund or World Bank handbook advising their staff on how to negotiate "most efficiently" with counterparts in Haiti or Sierra Leone.

Granted that there is a diplomatic culture, does this fact render other, even national, cultural differences totally irrelevant— or of only post prandial significance. Probably not, and for two reasons. First, it is not likely that one's most basic cultural orientations—what Fisher calls a "mindset" and we would call root metaphors or dominant, core schemas—can so easily be leached out with diplomatic training or enculturation. The reasons for this reflect the property we noted earlier as the psychological distributedness of culture—both in a population and "inside" an individual. Ultimately the reasons are psychodynamic. It is true that individuals carry multiple cultures, but the individual does not invest equally in all of these cultures. As Raymond Cohen put it: "No amount of professional training in later life can wipe away the deep-seated assumptions of childhood."[82]

The second reason to doubt the all-powerfulness of diplomatic culture is that this view overprivileges the position of professional diplomats in international negotiations. First, technical experts of one sort or another—military, scientific, engineering, legal— might dominate a particular negotiation; in which case, as Hopmann indicates, the more pointed intercultural negotiations might well take place on the same side of the table, that is, within a national negotiating team. Second, even in political or commercial negotiations, diplomats, regardless (or because?) of their cosmopolitan sensibilities, rarely get to shape their nation's foreign policy. Instead, the settlements they reach must be acceptable to the political (civilian or military) leadership and regime. The leadership is more or less responsible to the prejudices of the masses or to public opinion. Even if less than fully responsible to public opinion, the leadership is more likely reflective of the culture of the masses than is the diplomatic corps. This is true for

North America and Europe. It is true in the so-called Third World, where Oxbridge or Sorbonne-educated diplomats must answer to their leader, who is proud to be a "son of the village" and a graduate of an officers' training program—occasionally, a non-commissioned officers' training program: at worst, some Idi Amin Dada. Alternatively, some Idi Amin tires of his Stanford-educated foreign minister and appoints his village-educated kinsman to the post. And finally, as Raymond Cohen points out, whereas in negotiations around narrow or technical issues diplomats or experts who share professional cultures are more likely to predominate over politicians (at least until agreements must be ratified back home), and thus the effects of cross-national culture differences may be muted, "the more emotive, 'political,' and public the issue, the more likely are cross-cultural effects to be felt."[83]

In other words, it is precisely in times of international crisis, when the political stakes are highest and emotions run hot, that culture is likely to matter the most. It especially matters when the crises have to do with core cultural understandings—those, for example, central to the culture of diplomacy. It mattered, then, in April 1984 when shots rang out of the Libyan embassy in London, a British policewoman was killed, and the Foreign Office found itself in tense negotiations with representatives of the Libyan's "Peoples' Bureau." (What would Sir Harold make of Peoples' Bureaus in any case? How do snipers figure in an embassy's personnel listing? And by which cognitive model or schema of "fair-dealing commercial transaction" are they explicable?) Culture mattered in 1979 when Iranian students seized the U.S. embassy in Tehran and held American diplomats hostage. Fisher is no doubt speaking partly as a former diplomat himself when he characterizes the Americans' understanding of events in Tehran:

> That Iranians could defy all existing international precedent for respecting a foreign embassy was seen as highly irrational action. To Americans . . . [these Iranians] were viewed as primitives in a modern world. Just defining the action as an "embassy takeover" placed the perpetrators outside the limits of civilized behavior.[84]

Finally, we suspect culture mattered when Tariq Aziz returned from a crisis-meeting with James Baker—having refused to accept Bush's no doubt blunt ultimatum—to brief Saddam Hussein on the finer points of international law.[85] The first two cases, Libyan and Iranian, shook diplomats especially because both instances reminded them that no culture is timeless or, alternatively, that all cultural understandings—even diplomatic ones, say having to do with the "extraterritoriality" of an embassy or the "immunity" of its diplomats—are subject to precipitous reinterpretation in a protean real world. The last example, Baker and Aziz, suggests something else. Paul Kimmel has argued for the cultural dimensions—misunderstanding and misperception—behind their unsatisfactory meeting. But Baker's shocked reaction to Aziz's refusal even to convey Bush's letter to Saddam might also tell another story: that of a small country daring to thumb its nose at overwhelming power. This brings us to a third possible reason for ignoring cultural aspects of negotiations, international, intercultural, or otherwise—power.

Culture and the Problem of Power

Power trumps everything (including culture). With this third reason for ignoring culture we are in effect back to realist thinking in its purest form. To update the Napoleonic quip, God is on the side of the aircraft carriers, the stealth bombers, and the Tomahawk missiles. Even Cohen, who has written persuasively of interstate cultural misunderstandings as creating costly "dialogues of the deaf," agrees that the effects of culture are limited in any situation in which *force majeure* can be invoked, where, that is, the "power discrepancy between two states is so great that the weaker has no choice but to comply with the will of the stronger."[86] After all, how can culture, which affects the communication processes that are at the heart of the interlocutory conversation called negotiation, matter if the conversation itself is limited to the presentation of an ultimatum by one all-powerful party? Does the delivery of a command ever constitute a conversation?

Power is, indeed, an issue that has been addressed by various conflict resolution theorists in different ways, but most start out by pointing to some drawbacks of recourse to power politics even in the world imagined by the realists. The first question is appropriately a cost-benefit one. The use of power or force, they say, may indeed represent one "solution" to any problem in international relations, but at what costs (even to the stronger state?) and over what period of time (*force majeure* usually being more efficient in the shorter, rather than longer, term)? As Edmund Burke put it in his *Second Speech on Conciliation with America* (1775): "The use of force alone is but *temporary*. It may subdue for a moment; but it does not remove the necessity of subduing again: and a nation is not governed, which is perpetually to be conquered." Second, force used as a solution is used in lieu of what other solutions, solutions that are in the long run less costly and more likely to avoid future conflict? This second question, hinting at "other solutions," points us of course to the whole premise and field of conflict resolution.

There have been, as noted, different responses to the problem of power—or, more precisely, to the problem of a great discrepancy in absolute terms in one party's power over the other.[87] One response has been to acknowledge the importance of power and seek to redress power imbalances within the negotiating context. Note that this strategy, usually referred to as the "empowerment" of the weaker party, is undertaken by a third-party intervenor as part of the larger third-party processes aimed to facilitate the negotiation. (We have not yet considered third-party processes in any detail.) Some activists, such as the Quaker Adam Curle, argue that education is needed to increase the parties' awareness of structural inequalities and power imbalances. With increased awareness, *confrontation* can be used productively to redress imbalances.[88] Notice that this approach moves the role of a third party away from neutrality, because neutrality in the strict sense of the word would disallow a mediator, say, from trying to change in any way the preexisting statuses of the parties. Empowerment practitioners reject this sense of neutrality out of hand; indeed, their understanding of the third-party role shifts it into the domains of advocacy and activist concerns. We find this idea of empowerment more often in domestic, community-level, dispute resolution, particularly involving less powerful ethnic, racial, or community groups in dispute with establishmentarian (and deep-pocketed) entities, typically corporate ones or city hall.[89] But the issue of power imbalance has not been ignored in international disputes; it has surfaced in the specialized context of so-called problem-solving workshops (more on this later), most explicitly in the version of these imagined by John Burton, "analytical problem-solving workshops."

This other, more radical, response to power is to argue back at the realists, saying in effect: In some sorts of conflict, usually the most deeply rooted and seemingly intractable—usually, that is, ones having to do with issues of identity, nationalism, race, or ethnicity—power differences, even very large ones, do not in the end matter all that much. This position has been taken consistently over the years by John Burton in formulating his conflict resolution-based critique of power politics and realism.[90] The position derives from Burton's theory of conflict—indeed, of all social action—as being based on the frustration by social institutions of the universal, basic (and nonnegotiable) human needs of individuals. If their basic human needs are frustrated or denied expression, individuals will fight institutions implacably, even violently; and they will do so seemingly "irrationally"— against all odds.[91] Burton, like many others, has pointed to the American experience in Vietnam as a prime example of this phenomenon; others have looked at the Soviet experience in Afghanistan in the same way.

However, consider the Vietnam example from the arch-realist's perspective (or that of General Schwarzkopf or General Powell, who were junior officers in that war), and we can see why Burton's assertion that overwhelming U.S. power failed there and thus power is overrated (his case) is so hard to accept. Power theorists (and players) will always claim that failures resulted from applying too little power, from stopping the battalions too soon, from tying the hands of the commanders or calling back the B-52s from truly bombing the enemy back into the Stone Age. Thus, power theorists and players say, use *sufficient* power and any problem in the international arena is soluble.[92] But there are in the end two defects in this line of thinking. The first is a logical one: since all empirical failures of the use of force or power can be explained by the insufficiency of its deployment—indeed, the defining characteristic of failure is the insufficiency of deployment—then of course the theory is made all but impervious to disconfirmation. The second defect arises directly from the *practice* suggested to players by the analysis of failure as explained by the theory. As deployed by players, this defect is a moral one: use enough power and all problems are soluble (all conflict can be managed). And here we have a "solution" in the same draconian sense that genocide is indeed one solution to interethnic strife.[93]

Nevertheless, the challenge posed by power or force to restricted conflict resolutionists is a serious one, especially for those advocating some form of the problem-solving workshop. First, the idea that truly weaker parties can be empowered inside the workshop space is unproven. Second, we can argue that things might be worse if empowerment worked. The elimination or suppression of power discrepancy inside the workshop might resocialize weaker-party participants to unrealistically expect power symmetry to continue on the outside as well—and then they may find themselves in for some rude awakenings when they reenter their communities and the world. Many such workshops over the years have dealt with the Israeli-Palestinian conflict, and some critics, Edward Said among others, have pointed to just this very issue. Summarizing and generalizing their critique, Vivienne Jabri writes:

> While coercive mediation may be criticized for failing to change
> its power political base in its dependence on the use of threat
> and reward tactics for gaining concessions, the . . . [problem-
> solving workshop] facilitative approach may be criticised for
> negating power asymmetry in its discourse, thereby creating a
> myth of equals involved in unobstructed dialogue.[94]

We might add to Jabri's critique that in a way the so-called
myth of equals created by some versions of the problem-solving
workshop is not so different from the older myth of equals sustained by the culture of international diplomacy. What are all
the machinations of diplomatic etiquette and protocol and civil-
ity for if not to enhance a sense of equivalence among members
of a community who, however, represent self-evidently
nonequivalent states? Is there a better example of such a community of mythic equals involved in unobstructed dialogue than
the General Assembly of the United Nations? If we follow the
logic of this critique, then the only sort of empowerment that is
acceptable, and that matters, is one that alters power relations
not just in the narrowly defined conflict resolution context, not
just in the workshop, for example, but in the world itself. We are
asking for a world, or the sociopolitical institutions within it, in
which all parties, even the weakest, possesses the power of the
five Great Powers' Security Council veto. Here (realists will argue and we must agree), we are asking for a lot, nothing less than
a Galtungian transformation of the world.

To summarize, power, so central to the realists' view of the
world, remains problematical for conflict resolution theorists. In
facing the assertion that power trumps everything, they have in
the main responded to the realists on the realists' terms: by pointing to the costs of power projection weighed against its benefits
or, in some cases, even to the ultimate futility of such projection
of power against weaker though implacable parties in deeply rooted
(usually identity) conflicts. As we noted, the realists' retort to the
latter argument is simply to say that not enough power was employed. Another way of dealing with power, also on realist terms,

is empowerment, the attempt by third parties to redress power imbalances. The problem here is that, as critics maintain, such attempts are usually, at best, time- and location-specific, or, at worst, chimerical and ultimately *disempowering* (because, as myth, such attempts inculcate a false consciousness in the weaker party, and false consciousness, inimical to real social change, is usually disempowering). The only exception to this is if the third party uses its power by extension to empower weaker parties to the conflict—as the United States has done by offering security guarantees to a security-obsessed Israel in the various Israeli-Arab peace negotiations over the years. But this is just a Great Power's redirection of its power; far from challenging the power-trumps-everything assertion, it enhances it. Moreover, this sort of third-party approach to conflict resolution—where the third party contributes its power to the mix—is not what many strict resolutionists have in mind, particularly when they adhere to the maxim that parties in a conflict must "own their process" and find the keys to resolution within themselves or their relationship. A security guarantee by an outsider does not transform the essential relationship of the parties in conflict; it freezes it in place. If anything is transformed here it is the third party, which has now become another party *to* the conflict.

If power appears so recalcitrant for many conflict resolutionists, is it equally so for cultural approaches? Does the "everything" that power trumps include culture, as Cohen maintains? The answer is yes, but only if we agree that power is an indivisible, all-interpretation-stops-here entity, the simple *primitive* of the international (or any other social) system. Common sense tells us this is so. What is more emphatic and less in need of interpretation, after all, than the ability to deliver a blow to someone's head? But the rub is, Whose common sense—and whose head? Here are some questions with different answers depending on different common senses: What counts as a blow? How does one know when a blow is about to be delivered or has been delivered? And will blows to the head have the same social (as opposed to physiological) effects for all heads at all times? After all, the simplest accidental touch between outcaste and high caste can carry socially devastating effects in Hindu India—can count as a blow— whereas the same touch will pass virtually unnoticed, and almost certainly unremarked, among (Christian) Florentines or Floridians. In fact, common sense, even about power, misleads once again. Power is complex and never an existential primitive. At least we need to begin with Kenneth Boulding's insight that far from being monolithic, there are varieties of power.[95] We also need to acknowledge that power is never fully divorced from questions of legitimacy, and the bases of legitimacy are always cultural ones. Moreover, we need to acknowledge that the decision to project power is always part of a culturally constituted process of decision making, as are the forms of and rationale for its projection. And power projected *cross-culturally* is doubly constituted: once in its projection and again in its reception. Between projection and reception, cultural differences muddy the waters. The "clear" and "unambiguous" meanings of a projection of power often seem much less clear and much more ambiguous weeks, months, or years afterward.

Even while holding that power can overrule culture, Raymond Cohen, in his study of Israeli-Egyptian diplomatic and political miscommunication, provides us with evidence for asserting the opposite. Cohen considers why, throughout the 1950s and 1960s, Israeli deterrence, based on massive use of force as reprisals against Egypt for terrorist attacks emanating out of Egypt against Israel, failed to actually deter. Cohen considers the larger cultural understandings relating to violence, vengeance, and vendetta in the two societies. Israeli use of massive force violated Egyptian understandings of the conventions for vengeance and retribution; in particular, the Israelis misunderstood Egyptian notions of proportionality. The cultural logic of Israeli deterrence was that the "more disproportionate the punishment, the greater the victim's compliance. . . . Unfortunately [for both sides—K.A.], Egyptian rationality refused to conform to the Western, utilitarian model designed by Israeli strategists."[96] What the Egyptians regarded as highly disproportionate vengeance had the effects of shaming and humiliating them—a loss of honor. To erase the shame and regain lost honor, they had to support further attacks against Israel. Continuing Israeli reprisals ensured this support. The whole system of power projection and power reception—of failed deterrence—was part of a larger interlocutory encounter (where bullets replaced words), and it became a positive feedback loop for the production of violence. It was ultimately predicated, as Cohen put it, on Israel's mistaken "assumption that the Arab states shared the Israeli calculus of cost and benefit."[97] Here, Cohen undermines his own assertion that by exercising its greater power one state can always make the less powerful one bend to its will, rendering cultural factors irrelevant.[98] More important, by raising the possibility of a contemporary cognitivist redaction of *autres temps, autres mœurs* (other times, other customs)—of different rationalities and cost-benefit calculi for Israelis and Egyptians, he implicates culture as something central to the understanding—even—of power.[99]

Part III: Frames for Culture and Conflict Resolution

The focus of this part, which brings culture and conflict resolution into the same frame of reference, is mainly a methodological one. Concentrating again on international negotiations, particularly Arab-Israeli ones, we present two different strategies for making sense of cultural differences in "negotiation styles." One strategy is based on an actor-centered, thickly described, and context-rich—an emic—way of looking at culture. The other strategy is based on an analyst-centered, "objective," and transcultural—an etic—way of looking at culture. Both strategies bring with them benefits for conceptualizing cultural differences and intercultural negotiations, but in the end we make the case for not neglecting context, the heart of a cultural account.

Conceptualizing Cultural Difference

Earlier we outlined two different conceptions of conflict, one centered on scarcity and power, the other on perception or belief. It was easy to see that when culture is understood as ideational codes, schemas, metaphors, or cognitive models, there is an affinity between the perception/belief—the cognitivist—model of conflict and cultural approaches to conflict resolution, but that scarcity or power—broadly speaking, materialist—understandings of conflict would be less hospitable to such approaches. The epitome of such materialist and power-based understandings of conflict, we argued, could be seen in the classical realist approach to international relations and the state system. Our critique of the realist approach, and specifically of its use of the notion of power, was meant to question the deep divide drawn between cognitivist and materialist approaches to conflict (and by extension, to conflict resolution). One approach ought not preclude the other; but perhaps it is more important to argue specifically that even such seemingly "brute facts" as scarcity or power are not exempt from the interpretive lenses placed by culture between actors and the world. Or—if the sin of reification hangs too heavily over putting culture's role in that way (and it does)—we can say that actors think about their worlds, and problems in it such as power discrepancy, coercion, or social harmony, in terms of cognitive models passed on to them by others who have encountered these problems before. When two actors meet who have different models for recognizing and dealing with these sorts of problems, and when their respective models are backed up in their eyes by some special authority, authenticity, or feeling of rightness that may range all the way from ecclesiastical or sacred morality to self-evident common sense, *then* we may begin to speak of cultural difference.

Notice that culture appears as a sort of optical or perceptual illusion here: although always a presence, it can best be seen when thrown into relief by the quality of *difference*. For if two actors meet who share the same model or schema for dealing with, say, the power asymmetry evident between them, then culture is invisible, part of and buried in the deepest, and in this case shared, context of their encounter: Of course a Harijan stands when a Brahmin enters the room. It takes an outsider, one who does not share the same schema of millennium-old social and ritual hierarchy we gloss as "caste," to literally *see* (Hindu) culture, here. For Hindus, culture is invisible in this encounter because it is simply the way the world is. If the Harijan political activist refuses to stand (and increasingly, many do), or if the Brahmin reformer gently urges him not to (less frequently the case), then it is because either or both of them have imagined another, alternative world.

One reason culture seems to have infiltrated the study of international relations around the issue of negotiation is that international negotiations are where actors from different worlds encounter one another as interlocutors, and their differences become visible as the encounter throws them into relief. This is often more than a matter of difference in mere conversational styles, as Zartman argues. It is a matter of difference in respective definitions of what constitutes a conversation. To return momentarily to the domain of diplomacy, it is one thing to have a model of the ideal diplomatic encounter based on the schema of the British commercial transaction—"credit, confidence, consideration, and compromise." And it is quite another to model one on the image of a harmonious interpersonal relationship, a socially expansive notion of friendship, and a complexly manipulable set of dependencies and obligations implied by the first two—that is, the rich, embedded, and widely ramifying schema called in Chinese *guanxi* and analyzed in depth by Richard Solomon.[100]

But a very real problem arises when one tries to find a way to talk about these cultural differences, especially if the aim is to educate, train, or prepare individuals from one culture to work in another. The place to start is by avoiding from the outset the several inadequate ideas of culture that were discussed earlier on: culture as homogenous, reified, uniformly distributed, customary, and timeless. Instead, we should see culture from a situated actor's perspective. And we should see process over pattern. Now culture becomes less monolithic and more frangible, subject, that is, to the exigencies of change in a changeable world. An actor carries multiple cultures—national, confessional, ethnic, organizational, or occupational, to name a few—whose behavioral or motivational relevance also is situational and changeable. Not all actors, even in ostensibly the same social group or institution, necessarily carry the same array of multiple cultures (cultures are socially distributed); nor for any one actor is the psychological or motivational salience of a given subculture the same as for any, or all, other actors (cultures are psychologically distributed). This newer orientation to culture roots the concept more closely to the domains of ongoing social practice and experiential learning, where real folk live their lives. But it also has the effect of decentering or destabilizing the notion of culture by complexifying or "thickening" it. It makes it harder to use the idea to train or prepare individuals on what to expect in a new sociocultural setting, especially if the trainers are expected to explain what's out there in terms of independent/dependent variables, linearly arrayed in a monocausal and deterministic theory, or if training demands are strongly oriented toward the confidence-interval free prediction of a specific actor's behavior—something cultural analysis is not capable of.

Broadly speaking, there have been two main strategies for talking about culture—or cultural differences, to be precise—both of which can be found in the training- or practitioner-oriented literature. The strategies correspond generally to a distinction made in anthropology between *emic* and *etic* approaches to sociocultural phenomena. An emic approach is one that privileges an actor-centered understanding, what used to be called, in times less concerned with political correctness, "the native's point of view." An emic analysis identifies, systematizes (where possible or appropriate), and utilizes native categories, terms, and propositions about the world, culture, or the domain under study. By contrast, an etic approach privileges the analyst's understanding (or explanation) of these things. Native categories or thinking are of course collected and analyzed, but as *data* in aid of etic theorizing and explanation and not, as in emic studies, as ends in themselves. By definition, the aim of an etic analysis is to systematize data from different (emic) domains in order to construct (or discover—the verbs lead to different epistemologies) categories that work trans-emically. Over a couple of decades much ink has been spilled in academic debate and controversy within anthropology over the merits and defects of these approaches, a debate that continues today even if the terms themselves are less often encountered. For our purposes, the terms are useful as a shorthand, pointing to different ways of conceptualizing an approach to culture that has relevance for training negotiators or conflict resolutionists.

Emic Approaches

One hallmark of an emic approach is the identification and use of a native term or institution as the key organizing concept for description and analysis. A good example is Solomon's use of the Chinese notion of *guanxi* (ways of constructing interpersonal relationships) or *you-yi* (a sense of "friendship" that relies heavily on ideas of mutual obligation), referred to earlier. Another example can be found in the very large literature on Japanese culture, from Ruth Benedict onward, where the related ideas of *wa* ("balance" or "harmony," especially in a working team) and *amae* (an affect characterizing and binding individuals in an asymmetrical, dependency relationship) are often highlighted.[101] In a brief study of negotiating in the Middle East, William Quandt identifies two different indigenous models, each appropriate in different settings and with different actors. These are, respectively, the *suq* (marketplace) model and the *bedu* (bedouin) model.[102] Within anthropology, perhaps the most famous example of this sort of analysis is one that deconstructed not a word or phrase, but a rather curious institution: Clifford Geertz's "thick description" of the phenomenology and varied sociocultural entailments of the Balinese cockfight.[103]

The great advantage to the emic approach is that it roots the analyst more deeply (Solomon or Geertz) or less deeply (Quandt) in the relevant cultural context. It brings with it all of the strengths of ethnography: the attention to context and detail and nuanced translation. By focusing on the Chinese notion of "friendship" (*you-yi*), for example, Solomon is able to show how it differs from American understandings of the same term and, equally important, how these different understandings carry with them very different social or behavioral implications. Because his research was conducted (and disseminated) in a forthrightly political and policy-oriented setting, moreover, Solomon addresses explicitly how the notion plays out in official negotiations between Chinese and American interlocutors. He shows how it can thus be used in interparty manipulations of each other: deployed and countered in a series of moves Solomon calls "the games of *guanxi*." (By contrast, the more classical ethnographic uses of emic, thick description eschew—and probably disfavor—such manipulative strategizing.) The advantages of the emic approach for teaching or training purposes are self-evident, and especially so if used by individuals who will be posted to, or otherwise functioning in, that particular cultural setting. Moreover, much of this sort of description is amenable, if recast and analyzed further, to the sort of metaphor, cognitive model, or schema approaches we have been advocating.

The major disadvantage of this approach is that, in the proverbial wrong hands, it can slip all too easily back into thinking about culture in categories that we have labeled inadequate. At the very least, we need to have some sense of the sociological distribution of these key ideas in the relevant population, as well as their psychological salience for relevant individual actors. We need to be sensitive to the fact that there are undoubtedly always other, competing and perhaps even contradictory, models or schemas that interact complexly to "produce" behavior. We need to be cautious about imputing a timeless changelessness to these ideas. In sum, we need to be very careful not to think we have found *the* key that unlocks all the mysteries of American, Balinese, Chinese, or Japanese culture. The Balinese are not their cockfight in some metaphysical distillation (as Geertz would be the first to argue). *Wa* or *amae* are not all, or even most, of what there is to being Japanese.[104] These terms need to be properly circumscribed—kept fairly close to their main domain of relevance and rooted constantly in close dialectical examination of ongoing social practice, of texts or behavior (as Solomon does for *guanxi* and negotiations). When this is done, the emic approach is literally indispensable for a cultural understanding of conflict and its management or resolution. One version of this approach emphasizes the elucidation of the natives' own understandings and theories of conflict, and their own techniques or processes for managing or resolving it, what Avruch and Black call respectively ethnoconflict theories and praxis.[105]

In the eyes of many, however, a strength of the approach, its close connectedness to a particular cultural context, is also its major drawback. What good does it do to know all about *wa* if you are heading off to negotiate with the French? More generally, does a concentration on emics prevent us from making comparisons and generalizations that are valid across cultural contexts? Finally, isn't a concentration on emics in the end merely "descriptive" (a damning word in the positivist's lexicon) and thus of limited usefulness in the grand nomothetic task of theory building? The answers to all of these questions depend in part on where one stands with regard to larger epistemological issues in the social or human sciences; but among many who raise them a search for another, etic, vocabulary for speaking of cultural differences is a reasonable one. In the section that follows we will briefly discuss a few of the schemes that have been related specifically to negotiation or conflict resolution.

Etic Approaches

The hallmark of the etic approach is the identification of underlying, structurally deep, and transcultural forms, expressed in terms of certain descriptors that are putatively capable of characterizing domains across all cultures. These approaches vary greatly in their derivation and the sorts of data their authors feel they need to support them. Some of them seem to have been derived almost intuitively, after an analyst's wide experience of different cultures (an example is Edward T. Hall's high-context/low-context distinction). Others appear to have been derived deductively, by virtue of devotion to a particular theoretical orientation (Mary Douglas's grid/group is an example). Still others were derived inductively, after subjecting large numbers of responses collected across different cultures to aggregating techniques (factor or cluster analyses) designed to reduce them and reveal their underlying structure (an example is Geert Hofstede's work on national cultural differences). All of them claim to present the analyst with a seemingly universal scale or set of dimensions upon which all cultures can be placed and thus to present a vocabulary for encapsulating and comparing cultures across the board.

Perhaps the most widely used is Hall's high-context/low-context distinction.[106] The core of this distinction is a linguistic or paralinguistic one. A high-context communicational style (or individual message, for that matter) is one in which most of the information, or meaning, is "in the person" or the physical context within which communication takes place; relatively little is in the explicit and coded message itself. By contrast, a low-context style or message is one wherein most of the information or meaning is to be found explicitly in the coded message. In high-context communication, language use is expressive; in low-context communication, it is instrumental. High-context styles are rich paralinguistically (in kinesics, gestures, and so on); low-context styles are paralinguistically impoverished. In low-contrast interactions what you hear is what you get; there is a directness—often a rather assertive one—to communication. In high-contrast interactions, what is in the explicit message is rarely the entire story; much is implied and indirect and is to be found, as Hall puts it, in the receiver and the setting.

Hall is quite clear that high context and low context define

two ends of a communicational continuum and also that styles may differ within a social group, so that, for example, all other things being equal, communication within a family will tend toward being high context, and communication in instrumental, secondary, or task-oriented groups, toward low context.[107] But Hall also uses the terms as virtual dichotomies and assigns them to entire cultures: American culture, for example, is on the low end (but not so low as Swiss-German or Scandinavian); Chinese culture is on the high. Not surprisingly, the most interesting interactions occur when high-context styles—read "cultures"— meet low-context ones. Here the chances for miscommunication, misperception, and thus conflict increase. Moreover, if the interaction occurs specifically within a setting designed to limit or ease conflict—international diplomatic negotiations, for instance—then the effects of high-context/low-context miscommunication are exacerbated. Nowhere is this dimension explored more productively and convincingly than in the work of Raymond Cohen, both in his focused study of Egyptian-Israeli diplomacy (where such communication resulted in a "dialogue of the deaf") and in his more general work on diplomatic negotiating "across cultures."[108]

Hall's high-context/low-context distinction is not the only etic model available. In fact, by limiting itself to a single continuum or dimension, it is among the more simple ones. Several use two orthogonal scales. The social anthropologist Mary Douglas looks to sociological dimensions (rather than communicational ones) in her grid/group theory of cultural "bias," as she once called it: "group" refers to the boundedness of social units, and "grid" to the prescriptive forces that limit individual choice with respect to social role enactments.[109] Grid/group has been applied to explain a number of conflict situations, especially environmental ones.[110] The management consultant Wendy Hall, borrowing from earlier work by R. R. Blake and J. S. Mouton on the so-called managerial grid, identifies two behavioral dimensions that express all possible styles of negotiation: assertiveness and responsiveness (the degree of emotional expression or reserve).

Combining them yields four basic "cultural styles," which she calls the Compass Model, assigning to each a cardinal point.[111] Stephen Weiss (like Wendy Hall, concerned mainly with business settings but linked more explicitly in his case to national differences as well) identifies twelve cultural characteristics of negotiations, mostly on behavioral (rather than cognitive or sociological) grounds. He groups the characteristics into five main categories: the actors' basic conception of negotiation, their orientation toward time, their willingness to take risks, their protocol, and their decision-making style.[112] Finally, at the far end of the categories proliferation scale, some researchers in intercultural communication have come up with more than sixty etic characteristics, a veritable smorgasbord on which we can find just about any dichotomous distinction any theorist ever came up with: high and low context, shame and guilt, urban and rural, doing and being, and even the venerable and Benedictine Apollonian and Dionysian.[113]

Of all of these etic schemes, the one with the most methodological authority has been that developed by Geert Hofstede.[114] Hofstede did a large-scale survey for the multinational corporation IBM in which he examined work-related values.[115] He found that the values clustered into four major underlying dimensions or indices: power distance (the degree of inequality in a society, from small to large); collectivism vs. individualism; masculinity vs. femininity (his gloss for assertiveness and its opposite, say, modesty); and uncertainty avoidance (weak to strong).[116] In his more recent work a fifth dimension was added: long-term orientation to life vs. short-term. He noted that this fifth dimension did not emerge from his initial analysis of the data because of

> a cultural bias in the minds of the various scholars studying culture, including myself. We all shared a "Western" way of thinking. The new dimension was discovered when . . . [a different researcher resident in the Far East used a different] questionnaire composed by "Eastern," in this case Chinese, minds.[117]

The descriptive or heuristic advantage of a dimensional model like Hofstede's, located somewhere between the single continuum of high context vs. low context and the categorical profligacy of the sixty-plus schemes, is obvious: it is a very good way to make a "first cut" at aggregating and categorizing cultural data, including those that may bear on such aspects of conflict analysis as the perception of uncertainty and on such aspects of conflict resolution as negotiating styles. In general, the advantage of etic schemes is that they permit comparison across cases and thus the possibility for building theory. They provide for us a shared vocabulary for talking about cultural variation and diversity. For purposes of training or educating practitioners, providing such a comparative and generalizing vocabulary is a very good thing. Nevertheless, some cautions are in order, first, about Hofstede's work, and second, about the promise of etic approaches in general.

Hofstede's dimensional model is impressive as a way of talking about cultural difference; when he turns to examining some of the root *causes* of the dimensions—of social inequality or "masculine" cultures, for example—the work falters, moving uneasily between ahistoricist generalizing and mild environmental or climatic determinisms. However, cultural analyses have always been vulnerable to causalist mishandling. Perhaps more important—especially since Hofstede's model is the most methodologically rigorous of all the etic ones we have examined thus far, and such rigor allows Hofstede himself to raise this point—we must ask just *how much* cultural variation and diversity his four or five dimensions really account for. Here is Hofstede's answer:

> The four [dimensions] together account for 49 percent of the country [national culture] differences in the data, just about half. The remaining half is country [national culture] specific: *it cannot be associated with any worldwide factor*, at least not in the data I had. [Emphasis added.]

Charmingly answering the obvious follow-up question, Hofstede continues:

Whether explaining half of the difference is a lot or not depends on one's degree of optimism. An optimist will call a bottle half full while a pessimist will call it half empty.[118]

Methodologists will of course argue whether explaining 49 percent of the variance is a lot or a little—and it does, in a real sense, "depend." But we can also suggest, in a rough-and-ready way, that in the world out there any analyst who can adequately explain an admittedly complex phenomenon slightly less than half the time (or, at about the same level of confidence as flipping the proverbial coin) would not inspire much confidence in his clients.

Combining Emic and Etic Approaches

We cautioned earlier against proclaiming a particular indigenous notion or institution—*wa*, *suq*, *guanxi*, or the cockfight—as the open-everything key to any specific culture. If this is the besetting sin of emic approaches, then the limitations exposed in Hofstede's work should alert us to the waiting seductions of etic models: that we have found the even greater key for explaining (or certainly for predicting the behavior of actors in) all cultures everywhere. In some sense, the tension between emic and etic is related to the one we identified earlier as between local and generic understandings of culture itself. Emic approaches provide "thick description" and rich context. Etic models offer cross-cultural categories or discretely arrayed variables that, being scalable, are amenable to codings in databases and statistical manipulations; they seem to be able to reduce tremendous cultural diversity onto a few manageable dimensions.

But it is in their very power to reduce diversity that we find their greatest limitation. (This leaves aside the methodological question of how much diversity they are really explaining.) When the continuums are turned into dichotomies (as they usually are, despite the cautions of their authors), these schemes become very crude instruments for measuring rather fine aspects of culture. Moreover, if they lapse, shorthandlike, into reified essentialisms—

for instance, "Egypt *is* high context, Israel low context"—then one may entirely lose sight of all the corrections to the inadequate ideas of culture we have put forward. To review these corrections, first, cultures are mixes of all the dimensions—as are individuals!—and the dimensions are likely to be differentially distributed among individuals. Second, different domains, institutions, or social practices even within the same sociocultural setting are likely to differ in their dimensional profiles. Third, dimensional profiles may not be all that stable even within particular social groups or institutions. Fourth, and perhaps most profoundly, the very concepts that constitute the defining attributes of the scales—concepts such as "risk" or "individualism" or "authority"—*are themselves subject to cultural definitions.*[119] Finally, we must be very careful about attributing a specious causality to etic constructions, a sort of spurious prescriptiveness. If we have characterized an observable complex of, say, Egyptian or Israeli negotiating behavior as high or low context, it is logically questionable to then turn the argument around and say that some quality we now call high (or low) "contextedness" causes this behavior or that.

However, although we must always be careful about imputing causality, it is the case that a well-put-together typology or dimensional profile can help us to look for, even to probabilistically expect, elements of a cultural complex to hang together. For instance, having characterized Egyptian negotiating behavior as high context on the basis, say, of an expressive use of language, a rich paralinguistic repertoire, and a proclivity toward indirection—Egyptian negotiators hate to say "no" too directly—one is justified in looking for, and even expecting to find, an orientation toward negotiating that holds, in effect, that rudeness to one's interlocutor is a bad thing and ought to be avoided, even at the cost of what the interlocutor, say, an Israeli, may interpret as "insincerity." By contrast, low-context Israeli negotiators, for whom language is instrumental and unadorned with paralinguistics, and for whom facticity rather than rhetorical flourish is to be extolled, can be expected to—and do—demonstrate a certain directness and assertiveness in their communicational style (what Israeli Hebrew refers to as *dugri* speech).[120] Moreover, however much Israelis expect and appreciate *dugri* among themselves, *dugri* is perceived as rudeness in interaction with Egyptians, even if, as Cohen points out, the Egyptians are sophisticated and experienced diplomats. Conversely, the high-context Egyptians come across to Israelis (even to the sophisticated and experienced diplomats among them) as insincere or duplicitous.[121]

What then are the uses of etic schemes? First, they allow comparison, even for instruction across cases, and they enable efficient, retrievable handling of large amounts of cultural data. They can give us a good idea of what elements of a cultural complex tend to hang with other elements and, contrariwise, what elements we would be likely not to encounter. Etic schemes are thus a way to get at "first cuts," albeit potentially very rough cuts, of a cultural domain. But context ought never be sacrificed to the (false) efficiencies of aggregated data or one-size-fits-all theorizing. As an example, take the quality called "individualism" (typically arrayed in these schemes against something called "collectivism"). Nowhere does individualism exist as a monodimensional, undifferentiated quality—nor is the variation or heterogeneity simply a matter of more or less intensity on a scale. A complex quality such as individualism is always part of a dense cultural matrix of networked and interconnected schemas for cognitive understanding and motivated social action in the world. Within American culture, we can, for instance, speak about the "individualism" of the deeply believing or born-again Christian, for whom individualism parses because the individual is the ultimate locus of salvation and grace but for whom a crucial instrumentality of grace is the reaching out, the witnessing of the faith, to other individuals.[122] Compare this sense of individualism to the Adam Smith construction of it, the individual as a rationally selfish utilities maximizer, or the even more emphatic Hobbesian construction of the individual as an entity engaged in perpetual zero-sum struggles against other individuals in a nasty, brutish, and resource-poor world. All may be legitimately glossed by "individualism," and arguably all may share what Wittgenstein called a "family resemblance." But resemblance aside, they also are constitutive of different worlds as phenomenologically experienced and socially constructed by actors. To code all of these variations in a database as representing an instance of scalable "individualism" is to miss the richness and meaning that only a strong attention to context, to culture in the local sense, is able to convey.

Clearly, with respect to what we have called emics and etics, we need some nonmutually exclusive approach to linking culture with conflict analysis and resolution, the more so if we are to include cultural factors in the education and training of practitioners. To envision some combination of the two, let us take one more example, again from the Middle East.

Anyone who has observed Arab-Israeli negotiations has remarked on the almost obsessive concern of Israelis over the details of any agreement, and on their desire to have all possible contingencies accounted for in the final text (along with a general distrust of verbal contracts in favor of strongly written ones). This is related to the overwhelming emphasis that Israelis put on security. If we consult Hofstede's "uncertainty avoidance index," Israel does appear as a strong avoidance country. It ranks above aggregated Arab countries—and expectedly so if we have observed their respective negotiating styles and concerns.[123] Taking into account Hofstede's insightful distinction between uncertainty avoidance and risk avoidance—that sometimes we will take large (focused) risks to avoid more diffused uncertainties—we can even explain the Israeli tendency to take on such risks when they think their security is at stake. (Examples are the surprise attack of June 1967, the Entebbe raid of 1976, and the bombing of Iraq's Osirak nuclear reactor in 1981.) Now, clearly we have learned something from Hofstede's index, and a neophyte to the world of Arab-Israeli conflict or negotiations would do well to consult it.[124]

But it is only by careful attention to the Israeli context—to an understanding of history, symbolism, and psychocultural dynamics—that we get a real sense of what "security" means to Israelis. Security is connected to—*instantiated* in—a number of related schemas about the world that in effect enable Israelis to deal both with recurring situations and with unexpected ones. For some Israelis, typically the Orthodox, schemas may derive from a Judaic tradition that preaches "a people who dwells alone in the world" surrounded by implacably hostile nations.[125] For other Israelis, schemas derive from Zionist interpretations of such historical events as Masada or Tel Hai.[126] And for many, many Israelis, it is the European Holocaust that searingly defines the costs of inattention to national security. To understand the place of the Holocaust in Israeli political culture or political psychology demands a monograph in itself.[127] Our point here is more modest: to argue that any understanding of such etic a measure as "uncertainty avoidance" for Israeli society or polity ultimately demands the thick description and emic understanding of Israeli culture. And this, by the way, is not only a requirement for foreign analysts of Israel or third-party mediators to the Arab-Israeli conflict, but also for the various Arab interlocutors in negotiation with Israel[128] (most crucially the Palestinians) and, finally and not least, for the Israelis themselves.[129]

Put into the broader framework of Middle East conflict resolution, the purpose of such a deep, contextual—cultural—understanding of Israel's obsession with security is of course only part of the task. Another part would demand that now the Israelis undertake the same thick description and analysis of, say, the Palestinian concern with peoplehood and sovereignty.

Part IV: Discourses of Culture in Conflict Resolution

Building upon the methodological issues raised in the last section, we now bring together culture, conflict, and conflict resolution specifically to examine the way culture has been used or ignored in some classic conflict resolution techniques, from negotiation (starting with game theory) to mediation and other third-party interventions. The role of culture in the development of the analytical problem-solving workshop is emphasized. This is done because whatever the success of this controversial method—an important concern—it can justifiably be called the most innovative and audacious contribution to practice that the emergent field of conflict resolution has made thus far. With the discussion of the workshop, we highlight the work of two scholar-practitioners in particular, John Burton and John Paul Lederach. We do so not because they are the only, or even the most representative, contemporary players in the field, but because each strongly represents an extreme and opposed position with respect to the role of culture. Burton, recognized as primus inter pares among the field's founders, is the most prescriptive in connecting his theory to his practice, and the most consistently dismissive of culture in both. Lederach, who marries a religious sensibility and the concerns of some of the traditional peace churches with a program to go beyond conflict resolution to more profound social transformation, has given the widest role to culture in his so-called elicitive workshop approach. In the end, we argue that in any sort of intercultural conflict resolution, a cultural analysis is an irreducible part of the problem-solving process.

Finally, in the vein of practice, we turn in the essay's conclusion to the problem of education and training. Having addressed skeptics about culture throughout the essay, in this section we become skeptics ourselves, examining the limitations of "cultural sensitivity" training.

Rational Choice and Gaming

Culture can disappear from discourses on conflict resolution for several reasons. We have thus far examined in some depth one of them: a definition of conflict that focuses on divergences of goals relating to material interests and on the deployment of power or force as the means to resolving them. We have also spent some time critiquing this material/realist view. But culture has also been absent in some influential conceptions of conflict and conflict resolution that have sought to go beyond material interests or realist power politics, and it is to examining the bases of these that we now turn.

First, however, we need to consider, if briefly, one of the main ways for modeling conflict and conflict management that arose coincidentally to Cold War realist thinking about such matters. Specifically, it arose when postwar balance-of-power politics, having first exposed us to the possibility of mutually assured destruction in a thermonuclear holocaust, combined with realist thinking that sought to make it all seem intended and reasonable. In this discourse, "resolution" really meant "management," and the latter usually equaled "deterrence."

The theory of games as first developed by mathematicians was intended as a general theory of human behavior.[130] Soon it was adopted to explain conflict behavior[131] and then one sort of (broadly conceived) conflict resolution behavior in particular: negotiation.[132] Within the social sciences, game theory was developed furthest by economists, who found it a rigorous and thus convincing way to model (and "predict") individual behavior. That economists were sympathetic to game theory was not surprising: early game theory was purely derived from the rational choice paradigm, and the *individual* postulated by this paradigm—rational, calculating, maximizing of utilities—fit the mathematics, as well as the psychology, of both economics and game theory. Because these same qualities were imputed by international relations theorists to states, it is also not surprising that game theory was attractive to international relations realists.

From early on, too, game theorists sought to broaden the reach of game theory beyond the stringent parameters imposed by the original mathematics—for example, by moving beyond situations of "pure conflict" (zero-sum games where winner takes all and no consideration need be given to losers) to the mutual dependencies of so-called mixed-motive games.[133] Such development continues today. But as useful as the approach may be for modeling human behavior on the assumption of rationality, it ultimately suffers from the drawbacks of the simplistic and tautological cognitive psychology that the rational choice paradigm works under. First, the strongest forms of game theorizing (the ones that promise the best predictions) must assume that players—say, parties in a dispute or negotiation—have perfect knowledge of such key parameters as the rules of the game, ways to calculate utilities, or the probabilities associated with different choices or options. Imperfect knowledge of such parameters simply means that the players are defective—stupid, in fact. This hardly seems a promising basis on which to build a universal psychology for conflict resolution or anything else.

The larger problem has to do with the nature of utilities. In a sense, we can know about them only after the players have chosen them—behavioral choice then determines cognitive preference, and the tautology is complete.[134] We can assume a universal set of preferences, but then explaining the choices of some players who appear to have other preferences—those in other cultures, for instance—becomes problematical, as the Israelis learned when their strategy of deterrence failed to deter Egyptians (see above, p. 54). Or, we can admit that utilities can vary with context, thus admitting cultural preferences into the model but preserving its essential character of rational choice. This is the usual tack taken by those who see culture operating only at the level of "values" in a dispute (see below, p. 90). But including values does not address the generally attenuated psychology presumed by rational choice, nor does it give to context the full weight of its potential constitutive influence on the situation, on actors' cognition and affect. John Comaroff and Simon Roberts, who examined disputing and ethnoconflict theory and practice among the Tswana, point to the dilemma: "[Once the dispute] process is linked with utility—whether utility be conceived in terms of the universalist maximization of interest or the pursuit of indigenous values—it is a short step to treating the sociocultural context as 'given' and its relationship to the dispute as unproblematic."[135]

Bargaining and Negotiation

When social psychologists interested in negotiating behavior took game theory into the semi-real life of the laboratory, the most stringent (and unreal) assumptions of the mathematicians and economists began to soften. Indeed, many of the assumptions—the knowledge base of the actors, effects of other contestants on the psychological state of the actors, the environmental conditions of the negotiating situation, and so on—that were simply taken as given in gaming became the subjects of experimental manipulation and empirical investigation for social psychologists interested in negotiation and bargaining theory.[136] There was also the recognition that the theory must somehow relate to some real world of negotiation and bargaining, a world wherein it was plain that actors did not always calculate utilities in the manner of early Burroughs adding machines. Much of this real world data came from studying U.S. domestic labor disputes and negotiations.[137]

Nevertheless, the place of culture in the analytical social psychological approach to negotiation—and later in the prescriptive, "how-to" approach that devolved from it—has remained peripheral.[138] For the experimentalists, this is because the population they routinely use in lab experiments draws from the proverbial Introduction to Psychology 101 college freshman class. In fact, although there is likely to be some measure of cultural diversity in this group, we must look for it. In the mansion that is academic psychology, those particular rooms are to be swept, if at all, by cross-cultural psychologists, who reside somewhere down the hall in the next corridor (and who, themselves, end up using the freshman psychology class of, say, Haifa University, alongside Michigan State, as their cross-cultural comparative base). Finally, even in the small amount of work that has set out to look for cultural effects in negotiation, the notion of culture usually employed has been extremely thin—culture is simply the name, a label, for some sample of individuals who are subdivided among different nationalities.[139]

Alongside the analytical and experimentalist literature on negotiation, a huge, popular, and profitable literature of the prescriptive, how-to variety has grown up. The epitome is Roger Fisher and William Ury's *Getting to Yes*.[140] The first edition mentioned cultural differences not at all. In the second edition, in which a section has been added that addresses ten questions people asked about the first edition (rather like a rabbinical responsa), culture is lumped, in question 6, along with personality and gender, as a possible reason for us to adjust our Fisher-and-Ury–derived negotiating approach. The reader is given the brief menu of cultural characteristics from the larger cultural smorgasbord (slow or fast pacing; short or long time frame; low or high formality, etcetera, etcetera)—is told to "get in step" with it and basically not to worry—or to stereotype.[141]

The reason for culture's neglect in these works, especially those (most of them, in fact) written by experienced practitioners, is important. It is that the "theory" they propound derives strongly *from* their experience and practice. Earlier we wrote that culture is a derivative of experience, of the dialectical interaction between ideas and social practice: transformed by, and transformative of, both. In a more restricted sense, we can say this also about the small number of formalized (cultural) theories of practice that develop for certain domains—what are sometimes called in other contexts "expert systems."[142] Here, the proposition holds that *where practice is situated, there theory is derived.* And for conflict resolution, as for some other expert domains, the practice overwhelmingly has been culturally situated within a North American, male, white, and middle-class world.

Take, for example, Fisher and Ury's advice on dealing with affect and emotions in negotiations. Adopting their own sense of rational choice theory (where the efficient and principled negotiator remains calm and rational), they say that displays of emotionality are often unavoidable but that emotions (like seemingly nonnegotiable surface positions) are something that negotiators must get past in order to get to the real (often negotiable) underlying interests in the dispute. *Separate the people from the problem* is how they memorably put it. Let the emotions "ventilate" at the front end of negotiation, they recommend, always remember to see things from the other side's point of view, separate your fears from their intentions, but also keep your own temper—all good advice, in fact. But can we imagine a world where emotions and disputing are parsed differently, where separating the person from the problem, which in effect means separating the person from his or her emotions, is not conceivable? Here is Thomas Kochman comparing white with African American approaches to negotiating:

> In general, whites take a view of the negotiating procedure that is markedly different from the view taken by blacks. Though blacks regard whites as devious in insisting that emotions be left

in front of the meeting-room door, whites think that blacks are being devious by insisting on bringing those emotions into the room. [Whites believe that] . . . if the meeting is to be successful, the blacks' anger and hostility will be allayed by the results of the meeting. . . . Blacks simply do not see things that way. To leave their emotions aside is not their responsibility; it is the whites' responsibility to provide them first with a reason to do so.

It is not simply two different approaches to negotiation that we see here, it is two different sorts of social persons, for whom emotion is to be understood, and deployed, in two different sorts of ways. We can also see, here, the very real world in which power asymmetry is present and at work. There is little doubt, in negotiations over resources, who will eventually have to adapt to whose model if they are ever to get a "fair hearing." African Americans see this clearly. For middle-class white Americans, behaving calmly is simply the right, or efficient, or principled, way to go about things. For blacks, however, Kochman writes, "the requirement to behave calmly, rationally, unemotionally, and logically while negotiating is looked upon . . . as a *political requirement*— and to accede to it in advance is considered a *political defeat*" (emphasis added).[143]

None of this is to argue that Fisher and Ury's theory does not in some worlds make a lot of sense and in many worlds "work." Indeed, given how many copies *Getting to Yes* has sold, the theory clearly resonates with many people in many places. It is to argue, however, that Fisher and Ury's theory corresponds deeply to the *idealized* Anglo middle-class model of what negotiation looks like. (And like home-court advantage, to remind us that there is always political advantage to be gained by insisting on our own model to be followed.) The theory derives ultimately from a folk model—the privileged folks, in this case. These are the folks who "hold the cards" in many interethnic or intercultural negotiations; so it is not surprising that it is also their model or theory of first choice. In the end, by ignoring any consideration of the model's ethnic and class provenance, its promotion from folk model to expert's "theory" occurred totally unselfconsciously. And in suppressing the cultural dimension, we run the risk of losing at the same time a way to get at the asymmetries of power politics in intercultural negotiations in the real world.

Third-Party Processes and Roles

Negotiation is the most common form of conflict resolution (broadly defined) and for those, such as Anselm Strauss, who take a social constructionist view of society, also among the most common and robust forms of social interaction in general.[144] From the viewpoint of conflict resolution, however, negotiation appears to be a particularly fragile form. It requires that the two contending parties recognize their joint interdependence and be willing and able to remain in communication. But often one party uses the dialogue established in negotiation simply to coerce the other. Or negotiations may break down if the relationship between the parties is characterized by a large power discrepancy, by a history of enmity or violence, by previous failed negotiations, or by a general mistrust.

The fragility of negotiation is well attested to in the anthropological, ethnographic literature, which is focused on small-scale societies, as well as by our reading of world events in the daily newspaper. With respect to the ethnographic record, Klaus-Friedrich Koch provides an account of the Jale of highland western New Guinea (Irian Jaya). Interpersonal disputes there tend to escalate quickly to violence and even intervillage warfare.[145] Dyadic negotiations are hard to sustain and frequently break down, so that the next resort is usually coercive self-help. Koch ascribes this situation to the lack in Jale society of effective third parties, individuals who could "go between" the contending parties and facilitate their negotiations. In contrast, Evans-Pritchard's description of the blood feud among the Nuer of the southern Sudan provides a classic example of a third party who facilitates conflict resolution in the "ordered anarchy" of an acephalous tribal society: the "leopard-skin chief."[146] Especially in the event of a

homicide, where emotions run high and the culturally constituted demand for vengeance is strong, the leopard-skin chief allows negotiations to continue without the contending parties
having to meet face-to-face. He invokes other norms of Nuer
culture that militate against continuing the feud, and he offers a
way for both parties to save face by saying they have reached an
agreement only to honor the chief (or avoid his curse). Finally,
he provides a framework for the formal termination of the feud,
arranging for the delivery of cattle or other "blood-wealth" and
presiding over the final rituals of atonement. It is precisely this
sort of third-party role that goes unfilled among the Jale and in
much of highland New Guinea. Consequently, Koch writes, violence is endemic there.

Although cross-cultural research attests to the fragility of negotiation, it also upholds the importance of recourse to third parties (sometimes in the form of the entire community) as one of
seven key cultural features of what Ross has called "constructive
conflict management in low-conflict societies."[147] And it is worth
noting that the field or discipline of conflict resolution, especially in the more restricted sense of the term, has made the study
and practice of third-party roles and processes its major concern.
One thing that strikes the reader is that although the very large
"how-to" literature on negotiation (often coming out of business, management, or legal worlds) frequently has a contentious,
aggressive, or manipulative tone to it—"negotiate to win!"; "you
can negotiate anything!"—the burgeoning parallel literature on
third-party roles ranges, sometimes uneasily, from the social-
activist or agent-of-change, to the Solomonic, altruistic, saintly,
and therapeutic modes.[148]

Much of the literature has focused quite appropriately on the
diversity of possible third-party roles and processes. The fundamental distinction is that between some form of "mediator"
(broadly construed) and some form of "arbitrator" or "adjudicator." Both involve third parties as intervenors to a dispute or conflict. But mediation is really an extension of dyadic (or n-party)

negotiation; the mediator facilitates the negotiation process. The mediator, purely defined, has no authority to impose a decision or settlement on the parties. By contrast, the arbitrator or adjudicator possesses the authority to stipulate an outcome.[149] Thus, one defining characteristic of mediation is that it involves the *noncoercive* intervention of a third party.[150]

In looking at third-party roles and processes many legal anthropologists have compared mediation with arbitration or adjudication as procedures for conflict resolution or management. Most begin with the insight that in small-scale societies, in which individuals are linked to one another in multistranded ways (your neighbor is also a kinsman and co-owner of the family herds), mediation has much to recommend it. This is because mediation aims to preserve and restore social relationships by leaving the parties in charge of their own negotiation and its outcome, often mixing in doses of therapy as part of the process. In larger-scale social systems, in which relationships are single-stranded and their preservation is not crucial and in which the state coercively reserves to itself the maintenance of law and order (and defines a domain called "criminal"), adjudicatory procedures will predominate. In most complex social systems, of course, negotiation, mediation, and arbitration or adjudication coexist, and individuals use them selectively (when they can).[151]

In conflict resolution as a quasi discipline and field of practice, discussions of third-party roles and processes virtually never refer to arbitration or adjudication, even if these succeed in ending a conflict, but to some form, however modified, stretched, or critiqued, of mediation. The reason lies in the noncoercive quality of mediation. Any form of conflict termination that depends upon the power or authority of any of the parties, including a third party, to dictate outcomes cannot be considered conflict resolution "proper." It may well be conflict regulation, settlement, or management. But with imposed or stipulated decisions, one side typically wins and the other loses. Alternatively, the authority imposes a split-the-difference compromise in which both (or all) the parties may walk away feeling they have lost. By contrast, the promise of mediation is that both or all the parties, by retaining "ownership" of the process, can bring themselves to agreements (called integrative solutions) that satisfy all their concerns and that only these sorts of agreements will endure without the need to invoke or reinvoke externally based measures of compliance. "Coercive conflict resolution" is thus an oxymoron, a residue of realist thinking and power politics. For the most part, it treats symptoms, at worst, by merely suppressing them, and often with the metaphorical aim of allowing the attending physician to get some sleep. Rarely does it treat the underlying pathologies.

On the whole, the discourse on conflict resolution with respect to third-party roles and processes—especially when addressed to practitioners, and compared with the "how-to" literature on negotiating—has been relatively open to cultural concerns.[152] First, there has long been a recognition, especially by such scholars as Ronald Fisher, Louis Kriesberg, and Christopher Mitchell, that "mediator" is a complex term that covers many different sorts of third-party roles, so that potential variations on the theme (including cultural ones) are to be expected.[153] Second, because third parties in international conflicts often come from some European or North American country to work in a non-Western, or Third World, setting, cultural differences are more naturally highlighted. Finally, scholars or practitioners who have worked in or come from non-European or non–North American countries have consistently questioned some of the European or North American presuppositions that have been evident in developing practice.[154] Lederach, for example, examines the cultural premises of North American mediators from a Central American perspective.[155] Mohammed Abu-Nimer does the same from a Middle Eastern and Muslim perspective.[156]

One of the first American cultural presuppositions to be questioned—and note well that it nowhere appears as a simple dichotomy on any of the etic lists we considered earlier—is that the best mediator is completely impartial and unbiased, ideally unconnected, in fact, to the parties or their concerns. Perhaps this "ideal" can be approached in mediation as it has developed in American society, that is, often as part of the judicial system, attached to lower courts in alternative dispute resolution (ADR) centers. Here the mediator may not know well or at all the parties in the dispute; the mediator relates to them as a court paraprofessional. This now corresponds to the "single-stranded" social system discussed earlier, one that favors adjudication over mediation in any case. Moreover, studies have shown that these ADR mediators often come from a different class and socioeconomic background than do the disputants referred to them by the court; this can heighten the sense that the mediator qua middle-class professional can be impartial and unbiased to the (usually working-class) disputants [157] For whatever reasons—purely cultural ones like American notions of fair play and professionalism, or structural-cultural ones like class—the idea that the only possible mediator is impartial and unbiased was a very strong one in early theories and practice. More recently, however, some experimental work questions the supposed ineffectiveness of biased and partial mediators.[158] The ethnographic record in general does not support the existence of the uninvolved third party as either the norm or the ideal (and how could it be in small-scale, multistranded societies?).[159] Finally, scholar-practitioners such as Lederach and Abu-Nimer explicitly question the role that bias and impartiality play in Central American and Middle Eastern disputes. Lederach has coined the term "insider-partial" to emphasize the importance of a third party's trust by, and social connectedness to, the disputants and their conflict.[160] Interestingly, in an arena of third-party intervention different from the one we have been discussing here, the United Nations has found it increasingly difficult to uphold its old ideal of the complete impartiality of traditional UN peacekeeping forces, with respect to combatant parties, in the post-Bosnia world of genocide and ethnic cleansing.[161]

The literature on third parties in international conflicts indicates an awareness that understanding the intervention's *context* is crucial to its success.[162] Once context (alongside process and outcome) is considered important, the way is open for strong orienting statements such as that given by Jacob Bercovitch: "A successful mediation is predicated on the awareness of cultural differences and the creation of shared norms."[163] However, perhaps the most distinctive form of third-party conflict resolution—the one invented by some of the pioneers in the field and which, to some, has served critically to define the field—has been more ambivalent about the relationship of cultural differences to context. We refer to the problem-solving workshop, to which we now turn.

The Problem-Solving Workshop and Conflict Resolution

We referred to the problem-solving workshop earlier in this essay, when we spoke about the complications entailed by power discrepancy for conflict resolution theory and practice. Here we consider the workshop in its own right. The problem-solving workshop goes by different names, depending on the particular theorist or practitioner.[164] A third party (usually a number of people—a *panel* of topical and process experts) brings conflicting parties together in a neutral and unthreatening setting to help them analyze the deeply rooted or underlying causes of their conflict; to facilitate unhampered communication between them; and to encourage creative thinking about possible solutions—literally, to "problem solve." The panelists are not professional diplomats or representatives of some government or state, but rather are usually academics (and the setting often a university one). Likewise, the workshop participants are usually not official representatives of the parties in conflict, but rather are themselves academics, journalists, intellectuals, labor leaders, and so on (with, however, access to officials). For these reasons, the problem-solving workshop can be classified today as an example of so-called second-track diplomacy, that is, nonofficial diplomacy by influential private citizens that runs parallel to "first-track," official channels.[165] It should be stressed, however, that the workshop idea predated the articulation of second-track diplomacy and, in fact, contributed much to it.

Third-party consultations or problem-solving workshops have been used for conflicts in business, industrial, and human service organizations and in such U.S. domestic settings as community, racial or ethnic, or police-citizen disputes. But it is in the international sphere that the most important and theoretically interesting work has been attempted.[166] Moreover, the conflicts chosen have often been those least amenable to simple power bargaining over material interests. They have been conflicts between national, ethnic, religious, racial—that is, *identity*—groups over life-and-death matters of sovereignty, dignity, autonomy, group security, or outright cultural survival. Often the conflict involves an identity group (typically in a minority status) ranged against a state (often seen as "really" representing the interests of another, majoritarian, identity group). And because identity groups may sprawl across state borders, sometimes such conflicts have escalated to involve interstate conflict of the kind researched by realist international relations theorists. But these are not simply interstate conflicts over divergent material interests. Nor do they involve the sorts of situations wherein technical experts of the kind described by P. T. Hopmann for START or SALT talks gather with shared metrics to argue throw weights or downrange accuracies. Instead, arising from the turbulence of intrastate identity politics, they flow from a vast reservoir of potentially lethal primary-process thinking, with all the passion and unreason to which we alluded earlier. These are the sorts of conflicts Edward Azar called "protracted," and Burton, working from his theory of their etiology, named "deep-rooted."[167]

The history of problem-solving workshops reflects their involvement in just these sorts of conflicts. At different times since the first ones in the mid-1960s, workshops have dealt with protracted or deep-rooted conflicts in Cyprus, Lebanon, the Middle East (especially between Israelis and Palestinians), Northern

Ireland, the Horn of Africa, and South Africa. As well, a few workshops have considered conflicts dividing India and Pakistan, and between Britain and Argentina during the Falklands/Malvinas Islands crisis. There are several intellectual and practical sources of the problem-solving workshop idea. Among these are the Quakers, Mennonites, and other so-called peace churches, who have long been involved as private third-party conciliators in the sorts of conflicts we have mentioned.[168] Another source is in the so-called Yale group organized by Leonard Doob in the late 1960s and early 1970s. Doob used the sensitivity training-group ("T-group") approach, which focused on group process and had strong parallels to the quasi-therapeutic "encounter groups" of Carl Rogers. Doob and colleagues led a group on the conflict in the Horn of Africa (called the Fermeda Workshop, after the Italian hotel that hosted it) and another group on the conflict in Northern Ireland (called the Stirling Workshop, after its Scottish location). A third workshop planned for July 1974 on the Cyprus conflict was abandoned after the coup against Makarios and the Turkish invasion of the island.[169] But perhaps the most important formulator of the problem-solving workshop idea (and certainly the first to use it, in December 1965, when it was called a "controlled-communication workshop") was John Burton and the group he gathered around him in London (and later Kent-Canterbury) in the late 1960s and 1970s.[170] Some of his early associates in London included Christopher Mitchell and Michael Banks, as well as the Americans Roger Fisher and Herbert Kelman, both of whom ended up at Harvard pursuing different aspects of international conflict resolution. Fisher founded the Harvard Negotiation Project, and Kelman refined the problem-solving workshop idea and focused it on the Israeli-Palestinian conflict.[171]

What distinguishes Burton's approach to the problem-solving workshop in particular and conflict resolution more generally is the unique combination of his personal background (he had been the youngest head of the Australian diplomatic service before commencing a long academic career), his formidable strength of character, and his from-the-onset insistence that the practice of conflict resolution must be tied to, and rooted in, a more general social scientific theory of human behavior. Based on an uncompromising methodological individualism, the theory proposes a number of basic universal human needs, the number of which has varied in the course of Burton's writing, though "identity" and "security" remain key. According to the theory, the ontological status of these needs renders them unalterable and nonnegotiable; their satisfaction is imperative, and their frustration (usually by larger sociopolitical institutions) lies at the root of all (by definition) deeply rooted conflicts. This is so, writes Burton, because individuals will pursue the satisfaction of these "needs . . . regardless of human costs or consequences. Socialization processes and coercion do not seem to be able to control these basic drives."[172]

There are many problems with Burton's theory. In the citation above, for instance, he fuses needs with drives, and the derivation of the needs is unclear.[173] Nevertheless, the brute simplicity of the theory (most intractable conflicts take place among identity groups, so they must be about identity!) and its underlying dynamic—it is essentially a version of Dollard's classical frustration-aggression hypothesis—have made it extremely appealing. A variety of conflict resolutionists, for example, Kelman, use it as a touchstone even while their actual practice reveals a much more nuanced understanding of persons and conflict. Just how psychologically anemic Burton's theory is can be seen when we look at the more psychodynamically sophisticated models of third-party interventions proposed by Vamik Volkan or Joseph Montville.[174]

What most concerns us here, however, are the implications of Burton's theory of conflict for his theory and practice of conflict resolution. One implication is that the resolution of deeply rooted conflicts requires the recognition that at stake are not merely negotiable material interests but also nonnegotiable basic human needs.[175] The bad news is that such needs, by virtue of their a priori nonnegotiability, are not satisfiable from within the classic frameworks of conflict management, these being negotiation or bargaining (no matter how Pareto-optimally efficient the process), mediation (which is, after all, simply negotiation facilitated by a third-party), or, most pointedly, settlements of disputes rendered by authoritative third parties (whether arbitrators or more emphatic adjudicators). The last are especially inappropriate in deeply rooted conflicts because the authority always relies ultimately on power—force or coercion—and coerced settlements (which usually favor the more powerful, often establishmentarian, party) are rarely sustainable. (Recall that frustrated human needs will seek their satisfaction "regardless of human costs or consequences"; therefore the revolution will take to the hills or the suicide bomber.) The good news, however, according to Burton is that these ontological human needs, unlike material interests, are not subject to rules of scarcity. On the contrary, they are in unlimited supply, and their satisfaction for one party has the effect of increasing their availability to the other side. His prime example of this is security: increasing the security of one's adversary, even one's enemy, can have the paradoxical effect of increasing one's own security (presumably because the enemy will feel less threatened and have less need to attack, say, preemptively, out of fear).[176] Ergo, security, like the other needs, is nonmaterial. Therefore, a conflict resolution process that is based upon the parties' mutual satisfaction of their basic human needs can turn the usual interest-based, zero-sum (win-lose) solution into a needs-based, *integrative* (win-win) solution—one in which the basic human needs of both sides, or all sides, are met. His analytical problem-solving workshop is designed to be just such a process.

Culture and Problem-Solving Workshops: More Skeptics

One other implication of Burton's theory of conflict, one that especially concerns us here, is that it marginalizes the role of culture to the extreme, silencing it as effectively as does the power-based realist paradigm, which Burton so clearly opposes in most other ways. Culture doesn't matter because the basic human needs are generic (in earlier statements, genetic) and universal. At most, culture is to be found at the stratigraphic level Burton identifies with "values" (much like the earlier political culture idea of comparative political scientists). When pushed in response to critics, culture becomes the "satisfier" of the basic needs. Because culture is unimportant in the root causes of protracted conflict, it does not need to be seriously considered in the design of the problem-solving workshop. The job of the workshop panel is to help the participants excavate right past culture down to needs. In the 1987 version of his handbook for conflict resolution, in which fifty-six workshop rules are set forth, culture figures hardly at all. In one place, preceding Rule Thirty one, it is presented in the following way:

> Sometimes parties will come from different cultures and have difficulty over names. There will be introductions at the outset, but adequate reminders are necessary. . . . Place names are useful.

On the basis of this appreciation for the possible effects of cultural differences, the following is promulgated:

> Rule Thirty-one. There should be lists circulated of participants and panel members, and clear name displays in front of each.[177]

When the handbook and its fifty-six rules were updated and reprinted as an appendix to the Burton and Dukes volume, culture disappeared even as a source of confusion over names, and the relevant passage there, which refers only to panelists, not even to participants, reads:

> Panel members are likely to have different approaches, particularly if they come from different disciplines. They may have some difficulty in communicating with one another.[178]

Yet another reason for neglecting culture in these workshops relates to their strongly proclaimed *analytical* nature. In a sense we are back to the argument Zartman made about the universality of negotiation, but in the stronger form of the universality of human reasoning.[179] Many proponents of analytical problem-solving workshops believe they can discount culture because, as they assert, problem solving is a special procedure: it goes beyond negotiation and bargaining, which may be culture-sensitive. Furthermore, most of them contend, these workshops, although they involve a third party, have little or nothing to do with mediation; they are simply not about facilitating compromise toward the division and distribution of material interests among parties (what Zartman calls "50% solutions").[180] Instead, they argue, problem solving seeks integrative solutions and depends on analytical techniques that—assuming that people every-where *reason* the same way—render cultural differences ultimately trivial.

Two points suggest themselves. First, we need to look very carefully at the problem-solving techniques that are declared culture-transcendent and generic. Burton, for example, writes extensively of having the parties "cost" the consequences of their continued conflict. Now, it may well be that "costing" is a generic human trait, though it certainly looks best suited to a Homo sapiens who is mostly Homo economicus. And—as Cohen pointed out on Egyptian-Israeli understandings of retribution and deterrence—it presumes everyone shares the same cost-benefit calculus. Often, in an unreflexive way, our own ideas about the nature of persons, or the nature of human nature, end up determining the assumed "universals" of our theories, but, of course, such ideas may themselves be culturally constituted.[181] In fact, John Paul Lederach, who has functioned as a third party in several different cultural settings, has remarked on the power-ful uses to which indigenous poetry, proverbs, or storytelling can be put as part of a culturally expanded notion of conflict resolution practice. In a discussion of his mediation experience in Central America, he points out the cultural presuppositions that have privileged the very idea of *analytical* problem solving:

> Why is it . . . that in the middle of listening to someone give their side of a problem, I have a natural inclination to make a

list, to break their story down into parts such as issues and concerns? But, when I ask them about issues, they seem to have a natural inclination to tell me yet another story. The difference . . . lies in the distinction between analytical and holistic thinking. Our North American conflict resolution approaches are driven by analysis; that is the breaking of things down into their component parts. Storytelling . . . keeps all the parts together. It understands problems and events as a whole.[182]

Lederach's distinguishing analytical from holistic modes of thinking suggests the second point: that we ought to look very carefully at the presumed culture-transcendency of human reasoning, since what we find will depend very much upon how we frame the question. For instance, some anthropologists metaphorise culture as the problem-solving "logic" by which we reason our way through the world. And our conception of local culture, alluded to earlier, says in effect, other cultures, other logics. But if we assume that people everywhere reason the same way, then isn't there but one logic—and cannot analytical problem solving use that one logic? (This begs the question of whether or not "costing" is part of the universal logic.)

To answer these questions, we need to know about the cognitive psychology of human reasoning, an area of scientific inquiry that is still largely undeveloped—and even more undeveloped is the *cross-cultural* study of human reasoning. Nevertheless, two studies demonstrate just how mutually entangling reasoning and culture can be. One work examines the question of culturally specific logics, or "ethno-logics." J. F. Hamill compares syllogistic (categorical) logical reasoning and propositional-calculus logical reasoning in a number of cultural settings. In brief, he finds that categorical reasoning appears to look the same (though nowhere quite like the Aristotelian version of our logic textbooks), but propositional reasoning does not. Thus, if we take the ability "to do" a syllogism as the essential element of reasoning, then language and culture seem to matter not so much. The vistas for analytical problem solving seem endless—or at least, as Burton would argue, acultural (just get the names right).

But propositional reasoning, the logic that Alfred North Whitehead and Bertrand Russell introduced in 1910 in their revolutionary *Principia Mathematica*, which uses premises and operators from a semantic (linguistical) domain to compose arguments, is different, Hamill tells us. "Propositional patterns vary with language and culture because the semantic elements of the arguments mean different things in different settings. Those semantic differences can have both linguistic and cultural sources." Moreover, all logics, even categorical ones, ultimately involve the interaction of *meaning* with logical structure, to define validity—or "truth." Hamill writes:

> Meaning not only structures validity in human thought patterns but also defines truth. Thus syllogisms are structured in the same way from culture to culture. Yet the inventory of true categorical statements varies from culture to culture. Therefore it is possible for a valid conclusion to follow from a syllogism in one culture but to be false in another. Premises are a variable of culture in the same way as attributed causes.[183]

Perhaps the larger problem comes from having tied ourselves in the first place to thinking of culture as a kind of logic as understood by Aristotle or even Whitehead and Russell. Insofar as culture prescribes a logic, as we said earlier, we would do well to think of it not in terms of the crisp distinctions of traditional logic, but of the more hazy statements of so-called fuzzy logic, a logic for dealing with contingency and uncertainty. Nevertheless, Hamill throws us back onto meaning, and once thrown onto meaning, culture is inescapable.

The second work that considers the relationship between reasoning and culture is even more germane to our inquiry, since it deals with disputes and litigation over land claims among the Trobriand Islanders of Papua New Guinea.[184] Edwin Hutchins meticulously recorded and analyzed the reasoning used by Trobrianders to frame their claims and cases to see if these non-Western people reasoned differently than we do. Summarizing this rich and complicated book, the simple answer is, on the whole, they and we reason in the same way. But, the relationship be-tween reasoning and culture appears to be mutually constitutive. That is, while the Trobrianders seem to reason every bit as effec-tively as we do, their reasoning is inextricably bound up with their culturally very specific models about land tenure and the transfer of garden rights. As D'Andrade puts it: "The schema for the transfer of gardening rights contains a number of contingencies. It is these contingencies that Trobriand Islanders use in their reasoning. Their reasoning cannot be understood without also understanding these contingencies."[185] Once again, even while acknowledging that the capacity to reason is a human universal, we face the other fact that the representations of the worlds about which humans bring their reason to bear can differ profoundly from one another. Along-side meaning, Hutchins throws us back to representation and in-terpretation—back, once again, to culture.

To come back to the core of Burton's skepticism about culture and problem solving, what is universal seems to be that we hu-mans all reason in much the same way, for example, associatively, and in linked, prioritized, valorized, and networked schemas about the world. What is not universal, however, what is cultural, is what these schemas are about, as well as how they seem to be differentially linked, prioritized, valorized, networked by—and distributed among—individuals across many different sorts of social groups and institutions. To try to suppress this variance, even in the powerful setting of a conflict resolution problem-solving workshop, seems to be an invitation to failure. In fact, we suspect that this is not at all what these workshops—perhaps even Burton's workshops, bound by their imperious and ethno-centric fifty-six rules of procedure—are really about. The late Jim Laue, who had a lifetime of experience in practice as a third party in community, racial, and ethnic disputes, but who also was trained at Harvard in Parsonian sociology and was, therefore, no stranger to hypertrophied theorizing, used to quip, "Well, it seems to work in practice—let's see if it works in theory." In *practice* something different from what Burton thinks happens in a successful workshop may well happen—or at least something additional. In addition to, and alongside, problem solving and conflict analysis, we suspect that in a successful workshop comes also a modest bit of cultural analysis and even "culture-genesis." We turn to this now.

Reframing the Problem-Solving Workshop

We have used John Burton's model of the problem-solving workshop as our exemplar because his strong, indeed doctrinal, formulations of its structure, goals, and processes throw most of the assumptions of analytical problem solving into sharp relief. Many problem-solving practitioners agree, for example, with his assertive stand against using the workshop to foster better interpersonal relationships among the participants—the goal being to work on the relationship between the various identity *groups* (say) that they represent. (In fact, enhanced interpersonal relationships among adversaries or enemies may make the reentry problems of participants to their home communities more complicated, and even potentially dangerous.) This stand contrasts with the approach taken by some of the earlier T-group–based workshops. Not all practitioners agree with Burton's insistent advice that the third party (or panel) should never meet separately, or "caucus," with one side or the other. Burton absolutely discounts the contribution that experts on the area of conflict can make to the panel. On the contrary, because they are steeped in knowledge (and sometimes experience) of the peoples, culture(s), and history of the region, as well as of the conflict, their presence can be dysfunctional, he claims, as it is likely that the expert has already chosen sides. (Besides, as culture plays no real role in the etiology of the conflict, no one on the panels needs to know much about it.) Other practitioners—Kelman, for instance—disagree on this point; still others (Mitchell and Banks) seek some sort of middle ground in the knowledge that panelists, or some of them, should possess. There is a range of opinion about the benefits of single versus multiple or ongoing workshops and about the particular stage or point in the larger conflict cycle or process at which they can play the most efficacious role. Many practitioners see their relevance at all stages in the cycle, from prenegotiation to postconflict, whereas others, particularly those who adopt a "contingency perspective" to conflict resolution, stress their usefulness in the earlier (prenegotiation) phases, that is, in helping to bring the parties to the table.[186] Finally, many practitioners who bring a self-consciously religious orientation to their work see Burton's conception as overly analytical, economistic, and "cold." For them, conflict resolution must ultimately deal with restoring social relationships, and thus themes such as reconciliation, confession, repentance, forgiveness, and mercy—the stuff of "Truth Commissions," for example—come to the fore.[187]

All of the above indicates that while Burton's conception may represent the "strong form" of the problem-solving workshop, there has been significant variation in the form from the beginning, and there is considerable variation today. Compared with the archetype, most of the variants can be characterized by their relative flexibility with regard to rules and procedures, as well as their willingness to *learn* from participants and one another and to adjust their process accordingly.[188] There is also the sense, even while remaining opposed to working on improving interpersonal relationships, or committed to the need to get past the highly charged affect and emotionality likely to emerge at the workshop's first stages, that, equally, we are not just dealing with the transcendental and affectless "information/data processor" image of the perfect panelist that Burton conveys. (This is an image in which any panelist with any prior, substantive knowledge of the conflict is a potentially tainted and defective processor.) Even Mitchell and Banks, whose practice perhaps most closely resembles Burton's, begin their handbook with a definition of the third-party "professional" that (in a very un-Burtonlike way) stresses reflexivity and the potential for self-critique. "'Being a professional,'" they write, "involves, as a first step, making oneself aware of one's own goals and values in undertaking any problem-solving exercise."[189] To this exemplary advice we would add only that making oneself aware of one's own deep *cultural* presuppositions (such as privileging analysis over storytelling) is part of this reflexivity.

If Burton's conception of the role of the third party represents one pole—highly directive and prescriptive—then surely Lederach's conception represents the other. Addressing practitioners and trainers in intercultural conflict resolution, Lederach counterposes the prescriptive model of practice and training with what he calls the elicitive model. In the prescriptive model, one's own (typically North American and middle-class) presumptions about conflict and third-party roles are elevated to the status of expert system. The elicitive model aims to get at what Avruch and Black call ethnoconflict theory and practice, discovering, in the words of Lederach, the "models that emerge from the resources present in a particular setting and respond[ing] to needs in that context."[190]

Lederach does not so much discard the prescriptive model as he does disprivilege it. In fact, he thinks that the best sort of intercultural training benefits from combining aspects of both models. The prescriptive model may "empower" participants as they learn new techniques or strategies for dealing with conflict; the elicitive model empowers them by validating the relevance of indigenous techniques and strategies. It is equally the case that using the elicitive model helps the North American trainer by educating him or her to the possibilities of alternative practice and thereby enriching his or her own. Lederach is especially acute in discussing the relationship of culture to both models. The prescriptive model (contrary to the opinion of Burton) need not be dismissive of culture; indeed, there are many intercultural facilitators and trainers who boast of their "cultural sensitivity" in exporting their (North American) model. But because they presume that their "expert's" techniques are essentially universal and culturally neutral, cultural sensitivity in this case means, at best, translating the North American techniques into the client's language or, at worst, just speaking English more loudly and slowly. Culture here becomes, as Lederach puts it, "an additional level of sophistication and expertise added to the already trained."[191] In contrast, the elicitive model cannot be dismissive of culture, because culture is deeply embedded in the foundational assumptions of the model; it is part of the inherent context for theory and practice. Cultural analysis in the elicitive mode is not therefore a "value-added" asset to export-quality theory and practice—an advanced (and elective!) course in the conflict resolution curriculum. Instead, cultural analysis *is* practice—elementary, intermediate, and advanced at the same time.

Which brings us full circle back to the analytical, interactive, collaborative, problem-solving workshops. When they work, it is not just because a conflict has been broken down dispassionately into its component parts, costs and benefits arrayed on a balance sheet for all participants to compute. Rather, if they succeed, it is undoubtedly because, as Kelman and Rouhana write, the workshops "enable the parties to penetrate each other's perspective, gaining insight into each other's concerns, priorities, and constraints."[192] It is hard to imagine a better description of the exercise of an ethnographic imagination—or of a cultural analysis. We would go further, arguing that in *intercultural conflict resolution a cultural analysis is an irreducible part of problem solving.*

What does this mean "in practice"? Earlier, in pushing for a cognitivist understanding of culture, we advocated a view of culture as interlinked schemas, plans or scripts, ideational encodements and indigenous models and theories, and collected metaphors. A cultural analysis consists minimally of the setting out and making explicit of these things. A cultural analysis in the context of a problem-solving workshop is when, with the help of a third party, one party to the conflict gains some insight into the schemas, encodements, and so on of the other side—along with a clear understanding of its own. This is what we meant to illustrate in our earlier discussion of the Israeli obsession with security and uncertainty, as well as our look at some undergirding metaphors that some Israelis live by: the Holocaust, Masada, the nuclear arsenal as their "Samson-option." Some time ago P. H. Gulliver spoke of negotiations in terms of the parties' mutual learning and cognitive-cum-aspirational change.[193] Intercultural negotiations involve perforce intercultural learning, a much more difficult task, one that, as many conflict resolutionists have pointed out, can benefit from the help of a wise and insightful third party. But in the end such a third party must be aware that its task cannot be successfully accomplished if it limits problem solving to a culture-free version of rational choice theory, dynamized by an unreflexive version of the frustration-aggression hypothesis.

Marc Howard Ross, in his masterful synthesis of materialist/realist and interpretive/cultural theories in conflict resolution, describes the problem-solving workshop (among other techniques) in terms very close to our own. The problem-solving workshop, he writes, provides the parties with strategies for

> modifying psychocultural *interpretations*, a crucial step before effective joint problem-solving can occur in many polarized conflicts. . . . [T]he emphasis is on facilitating participation in situations that challenge previous *interpretations* of an adversary and offering the possibility of linking new information to a [psychocultural] disposition not emphasized before. It is hoped that new *metaphors* will develop, allowing adversaries to view each other differently, and that disputants may acquire skills that allow them to solidify and build on this change in interpretations.[194] [Emphases added.]

In this reframing of the problem-solving workshop, cultural analysis is part and parcel of analytical problem solving. But beyond that, what goes on in the course of conflict resolution (with the help of a third party or not) is the emergence of something like a new culture—a culture genesis. The new culture is a metaculture of shared schemas and ideational encodements, of understandings and symbols, by means of which the parties achieve a new image of their world and, as Kelman and Rouhana phrase it, a new "sense of possibility . . . that a peaceful solution is attainable and that negotiation towards such a solution [rather than a return to violent confrontation—K.A.] is feasible."[195] Of course, such a metaculture is fragile in the extreme, vulnerable to the stronger, better entrenched, and "traditionalized" old cultures—the cultures of conflict—shared by the participants' home communities or constituencies. This is why, virtually all practitioners agree, the problem of reentry for participants after *successful* workshops is so fateful.[196] And this is why, we would argue, for conflict resolution theory and practice to ignore cultural dynamics is to invite failure, for problem-solving workshops and beyond.

"Restricted" Conflict Resolution and the Future of the Enterprise

Earlier, when we first introduced the topics of social conflict and conflict resolution, we spoke of two different concepts of each one. First, we spoke of two concepts or definitions of conflict, one based on divergent material interests, the other on divergent perceptions or interpretations. Although a cultural perspective most easily fits with the latter conception of conflict, throughout this essay we have argued that even interests—and materialist or realist ways of thinking about them—do not escape the constraints of culture so easily. Even power, as we pointed out, in its usual sociopolitical manifestation as force or coercion, is culturally constituted. Even interests are subject to interpretation. This is not to say, however, that goodwill engendered by something warm and fuzzy called "cultural understanding" is enough, or that conflict is simply the result of a failure to communicate, say, between high-context and low-context interlocutors. Interests still matter. Even after mutual recognition, Israelis and Palestinians will have water rights to argue over for a long time, and some resources (like water in the Middle East) will always be scarce. Yet, the materialist or realist single-minded obsession with interests (as with power) is also not enough. In deep-rooted conflicts (often ethnic, racial, or nationalist ones), the parties will never be able to get to the point of negotiating interests (to "get to the table," as the late Jim Laue put it) until *prior* problems of perception and emotion—of interpretation—are addressed. And here we are in the domains of affect, language, and metaphor—of culture. In this sense, interests and interpretations are rarely mutually exclusive. They are not in a dichotomous relationship at all, but in a dialectical one. They interpenetrate, and never more intractably then when they are implicated in deeply rooted identity conflicts. In this sense, the difference between the two concepts of social conflict, materialist and perceptual, can be collapsed.

We also spoke of two concepts of conflict resolution. The first one reflects colloquial usage; it is inclusive, encompassing virtually any strategy or technique that brings a dispute to an end, or even stops the violence. The second, what we have called the restricted sense of conflict resolution, is specialized and exclusive. Rooted in Galtung's notion of "positive peace," Burton's notion of "conflict *provention*," or Lederach's notion of "conflict transformation,"[197] the restricted conception seeks to get at the underlying, root causes of the conflict, to solve the problems that led to it in the first place. Following the logic of this sense of conflict resolution usually means contemplating profound, even radical, structural changes to the sociopolitical system that gave rise to the conflict in the first place.[198] The restricted conflict resolutionists are unwilling to grant the broad or inclusive view of conflict termination the name "resolution." It is management, regulation, settlement, or mitigation. It consists of bargaining and compromise, of interest-based negotiation, of mediation, good offices, facilitation or—very close to edges of talk at all—of "coercive diplomacy." It may well result in signed agreements, cease-fires, demilitarized zones, truces, and armistice lines; it may even stop the violence and killing *for now*. But unless it gets to the causes of the conflict, to repressive institutions or the unequal distribution of social goods and resources, for instance, the agreements will be broken, the cease-fires will not be sustained, truces will not result in peace, and the violence and killing will assuredly start up once again.

Although we were able to collapse the first distinction, which is between interests and interpretations, by framing them in cultural terms, it is less easy to collapse this second one, which is between the broad and restricted senses of conflict resolution. Indeed, so far as the restricted resolutionists are concerned, much of what we have discussed in this essay, from diplomacy to gaming to negotiation and mediation, is not really conflict resolution at all. The real divide in the discourses on conflict resolution occurs here. Dialogue across these two discourses should be part of the agenda for the future of the field, both its theory and practice.

Right now the messages about this future appear mixed. In the late 1960s and throughout the 1970s, conflict resolution was a great hope. Some people even considered it part of a new social movement. By the early 1980s many people would adjudge the movement a rising success. The field was being taught in degree-granting programs at the postgraduate level, first in one or two, then many, universities. Alternative dispute resolution (ADR) was rapidly instituted in lower courts (and assimilated by the legal profession) and soon enough in corporations and the U.S. federal government. Mediators, facilitators, and consultants were abounding, and trainers were running courses and workshops to train them all—and one another. Professional societies were established, and soon enough people began to talk about credentials and licensing. Conflict resolution was becoming a profession.[199] By the late 1980s some practitioners would advertise themselves with "Have Process, Will Travel." Conflict resolution had become a commodity. By the early 1990s, after the collapse of the Soviet Union and the opening of Eastern Europe, it also became an exportable commodity.[200]

In reflecting on the apparently complete acceptance of conflict resolution in America in light of the above developments, it is hard not to recall Freud's reputed comment about the rapid acceptance of psychoanalysis in America, especially given the resistance he and it had encountered in Europe. The problem with psychoanalysis in America, he said, is that it was accepted before it was understood. At least, anyone with a commitment to the restricted conception of conflict resolution might think this way. The hopeful viewpoint is that, given enough time, perhaps even a more demanding, if not so remunerative, restricted sense of conflict resolution will prevail, one based on conflict *transformation*, aiming toward a profound restructuring of society and polity. But other evidence does not point to this at all. In the mid-1980s there was much talk about (restricted) conflict resolution as a "new paradigm" for theory and practice. By the mid-1990s, however, it appeared that the new paradigm was not so much still untried, awaiting birth (the hopeful view), as already declared too radical, utopian, or unworkable—and disposed of in the counterrevolution of pragmatism and "realism." Here is the influential Roger Fisher and his colleagues' view of paradigms lost and found, in their *Beyond Machiavelli*:

> Understanding our task as conflict management rather than conflict resolution is a paradigm shift—away from a conception of conflict and negotiation that stresses static substantive solutions and toward an approach that stresses the power of process. . . . The approach we discuss in the following pages gets results.[201]

Conclusions: Some Notes for Trainers and Practitioners

Talk about pragmatism, realism, and "getting results" brings us round to practice—and practitioners and their trainers—once again. What is the relevance of a sometimes abstract and theoretical essay on discourses of culture in conflict resolution for those who venture (or are pushed) into a multicultural world to try to resolve conflicts or, more modestly, to manage, mitigate, or regulate them? What is the relevance of this essay to those who find themselves negotiating or bargaining with cultural "others"?

Clearly, the essay's aim has not been to compile a handy list of dos and don'ts for the international traveler: don't offer your left hand to an Arab; don't pat a Buddhist on the head; don't expect the Latin Americans to be on time for the meeting. Nor have we been able to propose with any confidence a single etic measure that provides the theoretical or methodological key to unlocking culture's mysteries. We hope, however, that the reader is not left thinking that the idea of culture is so occult or mystical that it stands forever beyond our (hardheaded, analytical, empirical) conceptual grasp. It *is* graspable, but whether it is "operationalizable" in the usual, positivist's sense of this term is admittedly a different question. In the end, however, culture is much too important (we hope this essay has made clear) to be ignored because the usual suspect list of positivist methodologies cannot convincingly measure it or because the usual executive summary of policy "bullets" cannot easily contain it.

Raymond Cohen, in focusing on intercultural negotiation, has identified what he calls "Model C," or culturally sensitive, negotiators. These people are not necessarily scholars—linguistic, historical, or ethnographic—specializing in some particular region of the world; they are not "area experts," in the shared locution of the academy and the State Department. But neither are they simply "globalists" or "generalists" in the sense these two words usually convey: have cost-accounting system, will travel. Rather, says Cohen, first,

> these individuals are aware of the gamut of cultural differences and do not naively assume that "underneath we are all pretty much the same." Second, they perceive the potency of religious and other cultural resonances. Third, Model C actors grasp that Western rationality is based on culture-bound values and assumptions. Finally, they do not take for granted that an expedient (such as face-to-face negotiation) that works for one culture necessarily works for another.[202]

Our first lesson for practitioners is to second Cohen and urge that the goal of all training in intercultural conflict resolution is to try to turn out Model C practitioners. This does not mean that solid, substantive knowledge about the culture area one is to work in is to be shunned or avoided—it *is* a really bad idea to pat a Buddhist on the head. But it is to say that since most of us will never become area experts in many other areas than our own, and that the plane ride to Jakarta (even to Jakarta) is too short to learn all you really need to know about Indonesian Islam, you should at least be aware—*really* aware—that when you land you won't be in Kansas any more, and therefore that, as you enter your first negotiating session, such fundamental notions as deference, social distance, responsibility, and personhood will be different from those you have come to expect. This is only our old motto *autres temps, autres mœurs*, but deeply internalized and believed, so that within an hour or so you will certainly have learned the Javanese equivalent (in translation), "other fields, other grasshoppers."

Cultural sensitivity depends also upon having a clearheaded sense of what culture is and is not. Our second lesson for practitioners, then, is to review the six inadequate ideas of culture we discussed in part I of the essay. Culture is *not* a homogenous, reified, uniformly distributed, single-level, customary "trait list," timeless, or stable thing. To "know" an actor's culture ("he is Mexican") will not allow you to predict his behavior unless you know "all" his cultures—he's an engineer, educated in the United States, of southern *indio* background (remarkably), evangelical Protestant, etcetera, etcetera. And this is tantamount to saying that you cannot predict an actor's behavior unless you know the actor fully as a person, in which case you still might not be able to predict his behavior. (However, knowing someone's culture may well allow you to "predict" behaviors that are highly unlikely to occur, which prediction in the end might only come down to being astounded in retrospect!) The positive lesson to take away is that culture is much more diverse in its social sources (in its identities—national, ethnic, professional, gender, and so on) than a listing of passport nationalities would have us believe. Furthermore, cultures, not being timeless, are subject to change. This is a way of saying that the identities listed as social sources of culture are all potentially contestable and contested.

Cultures change because, as "derivatives of experience," they are responsible—adaptive—to all the contingencies that experience entails. Ideally, of all people, practitioners should have no trouble grasping the cultural perspective, because culture is fundamentally rooted in social practice. Culture is, as we quoted D'Andrade earlier, "socially inherited solutions to life's problems."[203] And the cognitive processes and structures we have referred to throughout the essay—schemas, cultural models, metaphors, and so on—all allow us to solve life's problems by assimilating new problems to old and trying old solutions for new problems. Or if that doesn't work, and we're still around, we can try to modify old solutions or invent new schemas or models or metaphors. Culture is socially inherited, which is why there is a traditional force to it; but at the same time it must be responsive to situational change, to environmental contingency and uncertainty. This is why culture also must be reinvented and revalidated by each generation, and nothing can be so out of date (and useless to the intercultural negotiator) as an old (say, five- to seven-year-old) ethnography, or an old (say, four- to five-month-old) embassy political cable, or an old (say, two- to three-week-old) intelligence briefing. There is a Moroccan proverb to this effect: "Men resemble their times more than their fathers."

Finally, as *discourse*, not as an adaptive product of human coevolution but as a way for us to talk about the world, culture is above all a way to talk about social, political, religious, economic, and psychological *context*. It provides us with a vocabulary for talking about the relationship of individuals to social groups and institutions. More abstractly, it provides an idiom for talking about complexity, incomplete systemicity, and change, as well as about interpretations, interests, power, justice, force, and coercion—matters that are also crucial to the discourses on conflict resolution.

In the end, the lessons to be learned for Model C actors are a little different for negotiators and for third parties. Intercultural negotiators will "learn" about culture because they have to, if they are to succeed. This is one reason academic lectures on culture tend to bore effective, experienced diplomats: if the diplomats are good, they know all this stuff: they learned it the way we all learn culture, by "inheriting" it (it's called "mentoring" in the State Department) and by experiencing it. At most, what a good academic lecture gives them is the vocabulary to articulate and make explicit what the good ones already know. The benefit of this, of course, is that once explicit it can be used to educate or train the neophytes, to shorten their learning curve. (But it is in the end no substitute for experience.) The other benefit, even for old-timers, is a more ambivalent one. It is that a cultural perspective, once learned, can be turned on oneself, one's own cultures, to examine, sometimes critically, the basic schemas, models, and assumptions under which one's own side operates. This is intellectually, and maybe even morally, invaluable, though in the long run it may not be, as they say, career-enhancing.

The lesson to be learned in adapting a cultural perspective for third-party types embarking on intercultural practice—perhaps most especially for the strict conflict resolutionists among them—is the lesson of hubris or, to put it into another discourse, the sin of pride. As to training, it is hubris of the worst kind to believe that a weekend of semiscripted role plays or simulations has one *thinking* like a Bosnian Muslim whose family perished in a latter-day concentration camp, an Israeli Jew who grew up breathing the air of the Holocaust, a Palestinian Arab who grew up breathing the air of the 1948 Calamity, or a Hutu or Tutsi with memories of rivers and bloated bodies. Perhaps if conflict resolution training is to make sense at all, it is less the training of cultural outsiders as intervenors, in favor of parties to the conflict, where the training itself becomes a specialized form of third-party intervention. And if this is the case, then of course the trainers have a special responsibility to recognize that the cultural aspects of the training process are crucial components of it, not a "module" to be added as an afterthought.

For the world is really a complex place, and one of the functions of culture—of cognitive things such as schemas or sociological things such as rituals—is to simplify the world so that we can act (not always reasonably) in it. To understand this function of culture is to get a handle on the complexity. But to positively understand culture, something practitioners and their trainers should aim for above all else, means never confusing the simplification function of culture for the world it represents. *The world remains a complex place.* This is our last lesson for practitioners. Here is how F. G. Bailey frames it:

> In the end the best conflict managers will not be cultural outsiders. They will be those for whom the culture is second nature. The enlightened outsider, laboriously searching for the relevant cultural constructs, has too much to learn. The willful outsider, who disdains the search and thinks he has a formula good for all occasions and all cultures, has almost everything to learn.[204]

Notes

1. R. Williams, *Keywords* (New York: Oxford University Press, 1983), 87.

2. A. L. Kroeber and C. Kluckhohn, *Culture: A Critical Review of Concepts and Definitions* (Papers of the Peabody Museum of American Archaeology and Ethnology, vol. 47, Harvard University, 1952). The precise number is 164.

3. E. Tylor, *Primitive Culture* (1870; reprint, New York: Harper and Row, 1958), 1.

4. E. D. Hirsch Jr., J. Kett, and J. Trefil, eds., *The Dictionary of Cultural Literacy* (Boston: Houghton Mifflin, 1988). This was followed immediately by a companion volume aimed at children: E. D. Hirsch Jr., J. Kett, and J. Trefil, eds., *A First Dictionary of Cultural Literacy: What Our Children Need to Know* (Boston: Houghton Mifflin, 1989).

5. Or yet another politics derivable from Herder's notion of cultural diversity and uniqueness (and pulling in quite a different direction from Boasian liberal antiracism): romantic nationalism.

6. Some have argued the politics cannot be partitioned out and thus "culture" should be abandoned and replaced with other terms, such as Foucault's "discourse." See, for example, C. Lutz and L. Abu-Lughod, *Language and the Politics of Emotion* (New York: Cambridge University Press, 1990), 9.

7. Raymond Williams framed this distinction and constitutive process nicely: everyone has *culture*, even though a socially delimited elite may also make claims to possess (the mimetic) *culchah*; in Williams, *Keywords*, 92.

8. P. W. Black and K. Avruch, "Some Issues in Thinking about Culture and the Resolution of Conflict," *Humanity and Society* 13, no. 1 (1989): 187–194.

9. R. Boyd and P. Richerson, *Culture and Evolutionary Process* (Chicago: University of Chicago Press, 1985).

10. C. Geertz, *Local Knowledge: Further Essays in Interpretive Anthropology* (New York: Basic Books, 1983), 16.

11. Indeed, for the first half of this century, most British anthropologists dismissed the American (Boasian) concern with culture to concentrate on the study of social relations. Their typical fieldwork setting was somewhere in the empire (usually British Africa) where, compared to Americans working mostly on Indian reservations and speaking with old men and women to "recover" lost cultures (recovering "custom"), they could, thanks to Lugard's indirect rule, work in relatively less shattered and still functioning social systems (discovering "social structures"). This advantage did not, however, prevent their own mass underestimations of—if not outright blindness to—the deep changes colonial rule *had* brought to these societies.

12. Not, by any means, that this wasn't subjected to strong anthropological critique at the time and, of course, subsequently. And interestingly, when Benedict in 1946 came to write her masterpiece of national character anthropology, on the Japanese, she found it necessary to use two (contradictory and metaphorical) descriptors for that complex culture: chrysanthemum and sword (R. Benedict, *The Chrysanthemum and the Sword* [Boston: Houghton Mifflin, 1946]; also *Patterns of Culture* [New York: Houghton Mifflin, 1934]).

13. Tylor was prescient. Scholarly reputations are still to be made by bringing the two, structure and individual, elegantly together again for the first time, a century or so after Tylor wrote; see, for instance, the many works of Anthony Giddens, notably, *The Constitution of Society* (Cambridge: Polity Press, 1984).

14. This section builds on material first presented in K. Avruch and P. W. Black, "The Culture Question and Conflict Resolution," *Peace and Change* 16, no. 1 (1991): 29–30.

15. S. Huntington, *The Clash of Civilizations and the Remaking of World Order* (New York: Simon and Schuster, 1996). By "civilizations" Huntington means an agglomeration of lower-level cultures (for instance, Egyptian and Pakistani cultures cluster and cohere in an Islamic civilization). Thus it is a sort of mega-culture concept of the sort we have discussed here, and it appropriately reflects mega-inadequacies.

16. For an introduction to the daunting mutual entanglements of language, talk, and culture, see M. Agar, *Language Shock* (New York: Morrow, 1994).

17. T. Schwartz, "Anthropology and Psychology: An Unrequited Relationship," in T. Schwartz, G. White, and C. Lutz, eds., *New Directions in Psychological Anthropology* (Cambridge: Cambridge University Press, 1992), 324.

18. Or something like the notion of subculture. There are ambiguities in the "sub-" prefix that need to be addressed in specific cases.

19. Among the most articulate and influential of these is Clifford Geertz. See his *The Interpretation of Cultures* (New York: Basic Books, 1973); and *Local Knowledge*.

20. On culture's differential internalization, see, for example, Melford Spiro, "Collective Representations and Mental Representations in Religious Symbol Systems," in *Culture and Human Nature: The Theoretical Papers of Melford E. Spiro*, ed. B. Kilborn and L. Langness (Chicago: University of Chicago Press, 1987). Spiro stresses affect and motivation; for a more cognitivist view on differential internalization, see R. D'Andrade, *The Development of Cognitive Anthropology* (Cambridge: Cambridge University Press, 1995), 229–241. See also Schwartz, "Anthropology and Psychology."

21. The most exhaustive discussion connecting experience to practice ("praxis")—and another solution to the structure/agency dilemma addressed by Giddens—is by Pierre Bourdieu, whose notion of *habitus* (mental or cognitive structures through which individuals confront and make sense of their social worlds) is close to what we mean by culture, or at least to cultural schemas. In Bourdieu's scheme, people are always unconscious of their habitus; our conception of culture does not require such unconsciousness, although typically much of one's culture may be beneath the level of conscious awareness. See P. Bourdieu, *Outline of a Theory of Practice* (Cambridge: Cambridge University Press, 1977); and *The Logic of Practice* (Stanford, Calif.: Stanford University Press, 1990).

22. D'Andrade, *The Development of Cognitive Anthropology*, 249.

23. L. Coser, *The Functions of Social Conflict* (New York: Free Press, 1956), 8.

24. J. Rubin, D. Pruitt, and S. Kim, *Social Conflict: Escalation, Stalemate, and Settlement*, 2d ed. (New York: McGraw-Hill, 1994), 5.

25. K. Avruch, "Conflict Resolution," in *Encyclopedia of Cultural Anthropology*, vol. 1 (New York: Henry Holt, 1996), 241.

26. On management and settlement (as differentiated from resolution), see J. Burton and F. Dukes, *Conflict: Practices in Management,*

Settlement, and Resolution (New York: St. Martin's, 1990). On regulation, see P. Wehr, *Conflict Regulation*. (Boulder, Colo.: Westview Press, 1979). On mitigation, see L. Kriesberg, "Conflict Resolution Applications to Peace Studies," *Peace and Change* 16, no. 4 (1991): 400–417.

27. There is no better place to start than Thomas Schelling's classic, *The Strategy of Conflict* (1960; reprint, Cambridge, Mass.: Harvard University Press, 1980).

28. And to his related distinction between "direct" and "structural" violence: J. Galtung, "Violence, Peace, and Peace Research," *Journal of Peace Research* 6, no. 3 (1969): 167–191.

29. J. W. Burton, *Conflict: Resolution and Provention* (New York: St. Martin's, 1990), 3.

30. J. P. Lederach, *Preparing for Peace: Conflict Transformation across Cultures* (Syracuse: Syracuse University Press, 1995), 17–19.

31. This discussion follows P. W. Black and K. Avruch, "Culture, Power, and International Negotiations: Understanding Palau-U.S. Status Negotiations," *Millennium: Journal of International Studies* 22, no. 3 (1993): 380ff.

32. The *locus classicus* of this view, for the twentieth century at least, is Hans Morgenthau's *Politics among Nations: The Struggle for Power and Peace* (New York: Knopf, 1956). The basic message has remained unchanged through the sixth edition of this work, published in 1985.

33. See K. Avruch and P. W. Black, "Ideas of Human Nature in Contemporary Conflict Resolution Theory," *Negotiation Journal* 6, no. 3 (1990): 226–227.

34. H. Morgenthau and K. W. Thompson, *Politics among Nations*, 6th ed. (New York: Knopf, 1985), 52.

35. M. Banks, "The International Relations Discipline: Asset or Liability for Conflict Resolution?" in E. Azar and J. Burton, eds., *International Conflict Resolution: Theory and Practice* (Sussex, England: Wheatsheaf, 1986), 10.

36. J. N. Rosenau, *Turbulence in World Politics: A Theory of Change and Continuity* (Princeton, N.J.: Princeton University Press, 1990).

37. See, for example, G. Almond, "Comparative Political Systems," *Journal of Politics* 18 (1956): 391–409; G. Almond and S. Verba, eds., *The Civic Culture: Political Attitudes and Democracy in Five Nations* (Princeton, N.J.: Princeton University Press, 1963); and L. Pye and S. Verba, eds., *Political Culture and Political Development* (Princeton, N.J.: Princeton University Press, 1963).

38. Morgenthau and Thompson, *Politics among Nations*, 147.

39. R. A. Rubinstein, "Culture, International Affairs, and Multilateral Peacekeeping: Confusing Process and Pattern," *Cultural*

Dynamics 2, no. 1 (1989): 41–61. This important paper prefigures many of the critical themes sounded here.

40. See, for example, R. G. Fox, ed., *Nationalist Ideologies and the Production of National Cultures* (Washington, D.C.: American Anthropological Association, 1990); and K. Avruch, "Making Culture and Its Costs," *Ethnic and Racial Studies* 15, no. 4 (1992): 614–626.

41. Morgenthau and Thompson, *Politics among Nations*, 151.

42. R. Benedict, *The Chrysanthemum and the Sword* (Boston: Houghton Mifflin, 1946). For a reading of it that underlines its subversiveness (the comparison at one point is to Swift), see C. Geertz, *Works and Lives: The Anthropologist as Author* (Stanford, Calif.: Stanford University Press, 1988), 102–128. Geertz calls it subversive because he notes that although produced as part of a wartime analytical policy effort to understand Japan, it was, like much cultural analysis, ultimately reflexive: a cultural critique. The book was also about American culture. This work has never been out of print, either in the United States or in Japan. In Japan it stands as a cornerstone of the vast body of literature on Japanese culture collectively called *nihonjinron*. Here it is read as proof of Japanese distinctiveness and uniqueness.

43. M. Vlahos, "Culture and Foreign Policy," *Foreign Policy* 82 (spring 1991): 63.

44. It shared this deficiency with structural-functionalist views of society, as well. Only recently has anthropology, in Eric Wolf's words, squarely "faced power." See E. Wolf, "Facing Power: Old Insights, New Questions," *American Anthropologist* 92, no. 3 (1990): 586–596.

45. As noted, this social contructionist critique of realism has grown in numbers and intensity. One work in the constructionist vein that attacks the positivist basis of realism, that is, the empirical validity of realist-derived hypotheses about the causes of war, is John Vasquez, *The War Puzzle* (Cambridge: Cambridge University Press, 1993).

46. This, at least, is one possible reading of E. H. Carr's *The Twenty Years' Crisis, 1919–1939* (1939; reprint, New York: Harper and Row, 1964).

47. Vlahos, "Culture and Foreign Policy," 63.

48. As we noted, however, they too must "psychologize" whenever they assume that social action is motivated; the question really is about the adequacy of the psychological theories that are ultimately used; and adequacy is rarely enhanced through outright denial of the usefulness of a theory you end up using.

49. A. Wendt, "Constructing International Politics," *International Security* 20, no. 1 (1995): 71–72.

50. R. Jervis, *Perception and Misperception in International Politics* (Princeton, N.J.: Princeton University Press, 1976).

51. Ibid., 8. Besides culture, Jervis also left out consideration of differences in individual actors' personality, what he called "ego psychology" and the entire problem of the "disturbed psyche."

52. It is by his systematic treatment of misperception, and his connecting it explicitly to such extant psychological theories as cognitive dissonance, that we make of Jervis a pioneer in this area. He is certainly not the first to have argued for the role of misperception or wrongheaded cognition as a motor of international relations and a source of conflict. See, for example, Ralph K. White, *Nobody Wanted War: Misperception in Vietnam and Other Wars*, rev. ed. (New York: Doubleday, 1970). For a more general look at inadequate thinking in historical perspective—indeed, it could be read as a broadside against assuming rationality in political actors *ever*—see Barbara Tuchman's *The March of Folly* (New York: Ballantine, 1985).

53. Uncertainty can take different forms. It can mean we have too little information. Perhaps this is why Aaron Wildavsky once called culture "codes enabling individuals to make much out of little" (A. Wildavsky, "Change in Political Culture," *Politics* 20, no. 2 [1985]: 95). But uncertainty can also arise from having too much information, and culture then becomes, as well, codes for enabling individuals to make little out of much.

54. These ideas are all addressed in D'Andrade, *The Development of Cognitive Anthropology*, which has the advantage in our case of never losing sight of the cultural issues in cognitive theorizing.

55. This is especially the case for the new so-called strategic culture studies; see, for example, Alastair Johnston, "Thinking about Strategic Culture," *International Security* 19, no. 4 (1995): 32–64.

56. P. Chilton, *Security Metaphors: Cold War Discourse from Containment to Common House* (New York: Peter Lang, 1996); also R. A. Rubinstein, "Cultural Analysis and International Security," *Alternatives* 13, no. 4 (1988): 529–542.

57. See, for example, G. Lakoff and M. Johnson, *Metaphors We Live By* (Chicago: University of Chicago Press, 1980); and G. Lakoff, *Women, Fire, and Dangerous Things* (Chicago: University of Chicago Press, 1987).

58. See, for example, J. Fernandez, ed., *Beyond Metaphor: The Theory of Tropes in Anthropology* (Stanford, Calif.: Stanford University Press, 1991).

59. O. Nudler, "On Conflicts and Metaphors: Towards an Extended Rationality," in J. Burton, ed., *Conflict: Human Needs Theory* (New York: St. Martin's, 1990), 177–201.

60. Or to map a simple domain onto a complex one.

61. A. Strauss, *Mirrors and Masks* (Glencoe, Ill.: Free Press, 1959).

62. See, for instance, R. Cohen, *Negotiating across Cultures: Communication Obstacles in International Diplomacy* (Washington, D.C.: United States Institute of Peace Press, 1991), 7; D. Pruitt and P. Carnevale, *Negotiation in Social Conflict* (Pacific Grove, Calif.: Brooks/Cole, 1993), 2; D. Pruitt and J. Rubin, *Social Conflict* (New York: Random House, 1986), 27; H. Nicolson, *Diplomacy*, 3d ed. (Oxford: Oxford University Press, 1963), 41. Negotiation also has been approached from a decision-making perspective, for example, by D. Druckman, ed., *Negotiations: Social-Psychological Perspectives* (Beverly Hills, Calif.: Sage, 1977), 41.

63. The difference between surface positions and deeper-lying interests—and the need to "get past" one level for the other—is at the basis of R. Fisher and W. Ury's enormously popular model of negotiation in *Getting to Yes* (Boston: Houghton Mifflin, 1981).

64. Thinking of negotiation as a mutual learning process is at the heart of P. H. Gulliver's sophisticated analysis of the process, in *Disputes and Negotiations: A Cross-Cultural Perspective* (New York: Academic Press, 1979).

65. Druckman identifies bargaining, influencing, and debating as "three cuts on negotiations" (*Negotiations*, 24).

66. This question is itself rhetorical; some diplomats speak self-consciously of "coercive diplomacy," an oxymoron (in the eyes of "restricted" conflict resolutionists, at least) located somewhere between blackmail and Cold War–style deterrence; see, for instance, A. George, *Forceful Persuasion: Coercive Diplomacy as an Alternative to War* (Washington, D.C.: United States Institute of Peace Press, 1991). For Druckman, coercion usually signals a crisis, and its use a "measure of last resort" (*Negotiations*, 28).

67. On Nicolson, see *Diplomacy*, 71. Catlin's definition comes from Chas. Freeman Jr., ed., *The Diplomat's Dictionary* (Washington, D.C.: National Defense University Press, 1994), 100. Napoleon, incidentally, had similar ideas: "Diplomacy is the police in grand costume" (Freeman, *Dictionary*, 97).

68. See, for instance, C. Jonsson, *Communication in International Bargaining* (New York: St. Martin's, 1990).

69. P. T. Hopmann, *The Negotiation Process and the Resolution of International Conflicts* (Columbia: University of South Carolina Press, 1996), 151–152.

70. In Nicolson, *Diplomacy*, 71, 77. Interestingly, one can see reference to (and reliance on) this commercial-transaction schema even in the more analytical, hardheaded treatment of negotiation by Fred Iklé, in *How Nations Negotiate* (New York: Harper and Row, 1964), 109, 145.

71. A sampling: Edmund Glenn (who was chief of the State Department's translation services), *Man and Mankind: Conflict and Communication between Cultures* (Norwood, N.J.: Ablex, 1981); Glen Fisher (a former diplomat and dean at the Foreign Service Institute), *International Negotiation: A Cross-Cultural Perspective* (Yarmouth, Maine: Intercultural Press, 1980), and *Mindsets: The Role of Culture and Perception in International Relations* (Yarmouth, Maine: Intercultural Press, 1988); and the various articles by working diplomats in H. Binnendijk, ed., *National Negotiating Styles* (Washington, D.C.: Foreign Service Institute, U.S. Department of State, 1987). There are also works by practitioners that deal with particular national negotiating styles: for instance, R. F. Smith, *Negotiating with the Soviets* (Bloomington: Indiana University Press, 1989); and R. H. Solomon, *Chinese Political Negotiating Behavior, 1967–1984* (Santa Monica, Calif.: RAND Corporation, 1995).

72. Again, a sampling: M. Blaker, *Japanese International Negotiating Style* (New York: Columbia University Press, 1977); L. Pye, *Chinese Commercial Negotiating Style* (Cambridge, Mass.: Oelgeschlager, Gunn and Hain, 1982); and R. Cohen, *Culture and Conflict in Egyptian-Israeli Relations: A Dialogue of the Deaf* (Bloomington: Indiana University Press, 1990), and his *Negotiating across Cultures*. Even the interest- and realist-based classic of the Cold War, Iklé's *How Nations Negotiate*, contains a section on the peculiarities of the Soviet negotiating style.

73. I. W. Zartman, "A Skeptic's View," in G. Faure and J. Rubin, eds., *Culture and Negotiation* (Newbury Park, Calif.: Sage, 1993), 17.

74. G. Faure and J. Rubin, "Lessons for Theory and Research," in Faure and Rubin, eds., *Culture and Negotiation*, 227.

75. Both quotations are from I. W. Zartman and M. Berman, *The Practical Negotiator* (New Haven, Conn.: Yale University Press, 1982), 226.

76. Zartman, "A Skeptic's View," 19.

77. Some time ago Erving Goffman called these "total institutions." See E. Goffman, *Asylums* (Chicago: Aldine, 1962).

78. Hopmann, *The Negotiation Process*, 144.

79. G. R. Berridge, *Diplomacy: Theory and Practice* (New York: Prentice Hall, 1995).

80. Fisher, *International Negotiations*, 8.

81. W. Lang, "A Professional's View," in Faure and Rubin, eds., *Culture and Negotiation*, 40. One such handbook is R. Sunshine, *Negotiating for International Development: A Practitioner's Handbook* (Dordrecht, The Netherlands: Martinus Nijhoff, 1990), esp. 25–90. Training programs for "Third World" diplomats exist in Austria and Switzerland; the University of Malta has run one for African and North African diplomats.

82. Fisher, *Mindsets*, 67–69; and Cohen, *Negotiating across Cultures*, 17.

83. Cohen, *Culture and Conflict in Egyptian-Israeli Relations*, 14–15. Again, properly speaking, Cohen means the more likely are cross-*national* cultural effects to be felt. What we are arguing is that cultural effects are always potentially present in negotiations, as any Washington bureaucrat or any Pentagon officer who has served on interdepartmental or interservice committees could probably tell you.

84. Fisher, *Mindsets*, 7. William Beeman has written on the key cultural misunderstandings of Iran's revolutionary regime from the Americans' side of the hostage crisis in "Conflict and Belief in American Foreign Policy," in M. L. Foster and R. A. Rubinstein, eds., *Peace and War: Cross-Cultural Perspectives* (New Brunswick, N.J.: Transaction Books, 1986).

85. For an interesting cultural take on the Baker-Aziz episode, see P. Kimmel, "Cultural Perspectives on International Negotiations," *Journal of Social Issues* 50, no. 1 (1994): 191–193. In recognizing the growing attention paid to culture in postrealist international relations, a number of case studies on the Gulf War explicitly examine the cultural dimensions of the crisis and the decision to go to war. See, for example, A. George, *Bridging the Gap: Theory and Practice in Foreign Policy* (Washington, D.C.: United States Institute of Peace Press, 1993), 42, 86; A. R. Hybel, *Power over Rationality: The Bush Administration and the Gulf Crisis* (Albany: State University of New York Press, 1993); and R. J. Pyne, *The Clash with Distant Cultures* (Albany: State University of New York Press, 1995), 93–130.

86. Cohen, *Culture and Conflict in Egyptian-Israeli Relations*, 15.

87. On the difference between relative and absolute power, and their effects on negotiations—mostly from the experimental literature—see Pruitt and Carnevale, *Negotiation in Social Conflict*, 130–132. On discussions of power in conflict resolution more generally, see L. Kriesberg, "The Development of the Conflict Resolution Field," in

I. W. Zartman and L. Rasmussen, eds., *Peacemaking in International Conflict: Methods and Techniques* (Washington, D.C.: United States Institute of Peace Press, 1997), 64–65.

88. A. Curle, *Making Peace* (London: Tavistock, 1971).

89. Much has been said about empowerment, but an orienting and exemplary statement of the reasoning behind it can be found in J. Laue and G. Cormick, "The Ethics of Intervention in Community Disputes," in G. Bermant, H. Kelman, and D. Warwick, eds., *The Ethics of Social Intervention* (Washington, D.C.: Halstead Press, 1978), 205–232; and J. Laue, "The Emergence and Institutionalization of Third-Party Roles in Conflict," in D. Sandole and I. Sandole-Staroste, eds., *Conflict Management and Problem Solving* (New York: New York University Press, 1987), 17–29.

90. A clear statement of Burton's theory (and practice) of conflict resolution can be found in his *Conflict: Resolution and Provention.*

91. Avruch and Black have questioned the ontological and generic (and genetic) formulation of these human needs; even so, there seems no reason to doubt the "power" of committed individuals to resist unbendingly the power of larger sociopolitical structures they view as terminally repressive—see K. Avruch and P. W. Black, "A Generic Theory of Conflict Resolution: A Critique," *Negotiation Journal* 3, no. 1 (1987): 87–96, 99–100.

92. Vietnam certainly provided Generals Schwarzkopf and Powell with their dominant schema for planning the Gulf War. One can imagine, in fact, that in the months and weeks before the war began, every time Saddam Hussein bombastically proclaimed that Kuwait would be another Vietnam for the Americans, the American generals would add another armored battalion to their battle plans. The lesson in this is that Saddam could have used some cultural analysis and advice for his dealings with the United States as well!

93. In its purest pure form, of course, realism rejects morality as being relevant to the *rational* behavior of states. (And a defining attribute of rationality is the absence of a moralizing calculus, needless to say.)

94. V. Jabri, *Discourses on Violence: Conflict Analysis Reconsidered* (Manchester, England: Manchester University Press, 1996), 155. The main force behind the Israeli-Palestinian workshop has been Herbert Kelman, who has written much on the subject, often in response to just these sorts of critiques. See, for example, his "The Problem-Solving Workshop in Conflict Resolution," in R. Merritt, ed., *Communication in International Politics* (Urbana: University of Illinois Press, 1972), 168–204; "Informal Mediation by the Scholar/Practitioner," in

J. Bercovitch and J. Rubin, eds., *Mediation in International Relations: Multiple Approaches to Conflict Management* (New York: St. Martin's, 1992), 64–96; and "The Interactive Problem-Solving Approach," in C. Crocker, F. Hampson, and P. Aall, eds., *Managing Global Chaos: Sources of and Responses to International Conflict* (Washington, D.C.: United States Institute of Peace Press, 1996), 501–519. Also see H. Kelman and N. Rouhana, "Promoting Joint Thinking in International Conflicts: An Israeli-Palestinian Continuing Workshop," *Journal of Social Issues* 50, no. 1 (1994): 157–178.

95. K. Boulding, *Three Faces of Power* (Beverly Hills, Calif.: Sage, 1989).

96. Cohen, *Culture and Conflict in Egyptian-Israeli Relations*, 97.

97. Ibid., 99.

98. Of course, because the theory of power politics may be made impervious to disconfirmation in this way, some Israelis still no doubt argue, "We didn't use enough power then! Or [alas], we don't use enough power now."

99. Perhaps Pascal, one of the inventors of probability theory and a man, therefore, who understood a thing or two about contingent relationships, said it even better: "*Vérité en-deça des Pyrenées, erreur au-delà*" (Truth on this side of the Pyrenees, error on the other) (*Pensées* [1670]).

100. The British ideal is taken once again from Nicolson's *Diplomacy*, 77. The "games of *guanxi*" are explored in Solomon's *Chinese Political Negotiating Behavior*, esp. 17–29.

101. See, for example, T. Rohlen, *For Harmony and Strength* (Berkeley: University of California Press, 1974), 47.

102. W. B. Quandt, "Egypt: A Strong Sense of National Identity," in Binnendijk, ed., *National Negotiating Styles*, 105–123. A neat comparison, showing subtle but consequential differences even within a shared (commercial-transaction) schema, can be made of Nicolson's British shopkeeper with Quandt's bazaar merchant.

103. Geertz, *Interpretation of Cultures*.

104. See S. Reed, *Making Common Sense of Japan* (Pittsburgh: University of Pittsburgh Press, 1993), 34–39.

105. In K. Avruch and P. W. Black, "The Culture Question and Conflict Resolution," *Peace and Change* 16, no. 1 (1991): 22–45; the approach is exemplified in most of the articles found in K. Avruch, P. W. Black, and J. Scimecca, eds., *Conflict Resolution: Cross-Cultural Perspectives* (New York: Greenwood Press, 1991). It parallels the work of John Paul Lederach, who has developed it further for training purposes.

106. Presented most fully in E. T. Hall, *Beyond Culture* (New York: Anchor Books, 1976); but see also his classic *The Silent Language* (New York: Doubleday, 1959).

107. Aspects of high and low context are reproduced in Basil Bernstein's more narrowly sociolinguistic notion of "restricted" (high-context: closed and status-oriented) codes and "elaborated" (low-context: open-ended and person-oriented) codes, a notion much used in education-research, especially in ethnographies of ethnic and class conflict in the classroom setting. See B. Bernstein, "Elaborated and Restricted Codes: Their Social Origins and Consequences," in J. Gumperz and D. Hymes, eds., "The Ethnography of Communication," *American Anthropologist* 66, no. 6, pt. 2 (1964): 55–69.

108. Cohen, *Culture and Conflict in Egyptian-Israeli Relations* and *Negotiating across Cultures*.

109. Mary Douglas, *Natural Symbols: Explorations in Cosmology*, 2d ed. (London: Routledge, 1996).

110. See, for example, M. Douglas and A. Wildavsky, *Risk and Culture: An Essay on the Selection of Technological and Environmental Dangers* (Berkeley: University of California Press, 1982).

111. North: low-assertive, low-responsive; South: high-assertive, high-responsive; East: low-assertive, high-responsive; and West: high-assertive, low-responsive. See W. Hall, *Managing Cultures: Making Strategic Relationships Work* (New York: Wiley, 1995), 50ff. Hall is more interested in organizational cultures than in national ones (though she claims her model is perfectly adequate for national ones, too), and her treatment, as are many in the business or management literature— and, one suspects, in the classified government or intelligence literature on national negotiating styles—is very instrumental in tone and aim: how to know the other so as better to manipulate the other (and resist being manipulated in turn). On the managerial grid, see R. R. Blake and J. S. Mouton, *The Managerial Grid* (Houston: Gulf Publishing, 1964).

112. S. Weiss, "Negotiating with Romans, Part I," *Sloan Management Review* 35, no. 2 (1994): 51–61. Weiss's scheme has been used in the business-oriented literature, for instance in the popular handbook aimed at intercultural managers, P. Harris and R. Moran, *Managing Cultural Differences*, 4th ed. (Houston: Gulf Publishing, 1996), 45–46.

113. G. Weaver, *Culture, Communication, and Conflict* (Needham Heights, Mass.: Ginn Press, 1994), 45–47.

114. First, in G. Hofstede, *Culture's Consequences: International Differences in Work-Related Values* (Beverly Hills, Calif.: Sage, 1980); more recently in G. Hofstede, *Cultures and Organizations: Software of the Mind* (New York: McGraw-Hill, 1991).

115. Two surveys were done, one in 1968 and the other in 1972. According to Hofstede, the database comprised about 116,000 questionnaires from employees in 72 IBM subsidiaries, across 38 different occupations and 20 languages, from more than 50 countries.

116. Hofstede makes a point of differentiating "uncertainty" from "risk" (cf. Weiss). Uncertainty is a free-floating and diffuse anxiety about the world in general; risk is a focused fear about the probability of occurrence of a specific (and negative) event. Uncertainty avoidance is directed mostly toward the reduction of ambiguity or ambiguous situations; Hofstede argues (correctly) that individuals may in fact engage in highly risky behavior—such as picking a fight with a powerful opponent—if they think it will reduce ambiguity.

117. Hofstede, *Cultures and Organizations*, 14–15.

118. Ibid., 252.

119. This is why, Hofstede insightfully tells us, he missed the fifth dimension, the length-of-term orientation toward life, in his initial reduction of the voluminous values data; the dimension was not "inside" his "Western" mind, to begin with.

120. See T. Katriel, *Talking Straight: "Dugri" Speech in Israeli Sabra Culture* (Cambridge: Cambridge University Press, 1986).

121. A caveat about the different typologies or models is in order here. Although Hall's high-context/low-context model "predicts" that Israelis will be perceived as rude, assertive, and less concerned about the maintenance of social relationships than their high-context Egyptian interlocutors, in Hofstede's model Arab countries (lumped together, including Egypt) actually rank higher than Israel does on the "masculinity index," which measures degree of assertiveness, concern with relationships, and so on. (Out of fifty-three ranked countries, Israel ranked twenty-ninth, Arab countries twenty-third.) Despite a sense, strong in Hofstede's later work, that most of these etic schemes are getting at different parts of the same elephant—as do E. Hall's and Basil Bernstein's—the question of intertypology reliability is open and unexplored.

122. For cultural unpacking of this sense of individualism, see C. Greenhouse, *Praying for Justice: Faith, Order, and Community in an American Town* (Ithaca, N.Y.: Cornell University Press, 1986).

123. Of fifty-three ranked countries, Israel is nineteenth, Arab countries twenty-seventh.

124. Costa Rica, however, a country that has managed to do away with its army despite its tumultuous Central American surroundings, ranks higher than Israel by several notches in uncertainty avoidance. One presumes that the explanation for this apparent paradox lies in a deeper exploration of the Costa Rican context, if not in some defect in the design of Hofstede's model.

125. Although he relies on the more traditional idea of ideology rather than schema or cognitive model, Ian Lustick sets out the world view of the Nationalist Orthodox and their construal of Judaism clearly in his *For the Land and the Lord: Jewish Fundamentalism in Israel* (New York: Council on Foreign Relations, 1988).

126. See, for example, N. Ben-Yehuda, *The Masada Myth: Collective Memory and Mythmaking in Israel* (Madison: University of Wisconsin Press, 1995); and more generally, Y. Zerubavel, *Recovered Roots: Collective Memory and the Making of Israeli National Tradition* (Chicago: University of Chicago Press, 1995).

127. Start with Menachem Begin's autobiography, *The Revolt* (New York: Nash, 1977).

128. As for the Arabs, many commentators, including Cohen, have written about the Arabs' massive misunderstanding, in the weeks before the June 1967 war, of the powerful effects their ("high-context") genocidal rhetoric (especially on the radio) had on Israelis, by whom it was "schematized"—cognized and acting as a behavioral motivator—in terms of the Holocaust (and prescribing, for many Israelis, its major motivational lesson: "Never again!").

129. As for the Israelis: Masada, after all, ended in the Jewish resistors' mass suicide when facing imminent defeat by the Romans. It is not then surprising (but hardly hopeful or reassuring) that the Israeli nuclear option has been called the "Masada option." Some of the possible outcomes of using Masada as a schema for action are explored by Y. Harkabi in his *The Bar Kokhba Syndrome: Risk and Realism in International Relations* (New York: Rossel Books, 1982). (Bar Kokhba was a Zealot leader on Masada, and reputedly the organizer of the suicide.) Avner Cohen (personal communication) notes that former Prime Minister Levi Eshkol referred to Israel's bomb as the "Samson option," a biblical metaphor whose accompanying schema is at once terrifying and depressing.

130. J. von Neumann and O. Morgenstern, *Theory of Games and Economic Behavior* (Princeton, N.J.: Princeton University Press, 1944).

131. A. Rapoport, *Fights, Games, and Debates* (Ann Arbor: University of Michigan Press, 1960).

132. H. Raiffa, *The Art and Science of Negotiation* (Cambridge, Mass.: Harvard University Press, 1982).

133. See, for instance, T. Schelling in *The Strategy of Conflict* (Cambridge, Mass.: Harvard University Press, 1960), 83ff.

134. Of course, a very similar tautology supported the entire edifice of classical behaviorism in academic psychology for a long time.

135. J. Comaroff and S. Roberts, *Rules and Processes: The Cultural Context of Dispute in an African Context* (Chicago: University of Chicago Press, 1981), 17. See also Avruch and Black, "Ideas of Human Nature," 221–228.

136. See, for example, Druckman, *Negotiations*; and D. Pruitt, *Negotiation Behavior* (New York: Academic Press, 1981).

137. See especially R. Walton and R. McKersie, *A Behavioral Theory of Labor Negotiations* (New York: McGraw-Hill, 1965).

138. For instance, a recent and comprehensive review of work done, mainly in the experimental field, devotes barely two (out of about two hundred) pages to culture, in a concluding section called "prospects for future research." Alas, this fairly reflects the amount of substantive work done by experimentalists. Pruitt and Carnevale, *Negotiation in Social Conflict*, 197–198.

139. See, for example, D. Druckman et al., "Cultural Differences in Bargaining Behavior: India, Argentina, and the United States," *Journal of Conflict Resolution* 20 (1976): 413–452.

140. Fisher and Ury, *Getting to Yes*.

141. R. Fisher, W. Ury, and B. Patton, *Getting to Yes*, 2d ed. (Boston: Houghton Mifflin, 1991), 166–168. To be fair, readers are also told, more helpfully, to "question their assumptions."

142. D'Andrade distinguishes "cultural models" as interrelated sets of schemas from "cultural theories" as interrelated sets of propositions, on the basis that the former are implicit and unvoiced—though not unvoiceable; the latter are formalized and explicit; see D'Andrade, *The Development of Cognitive Anthropology*, 172–173.

143. Both citations from T. Kochman, *Black and White Styles in Conflict* (Chicago: University of Chicago Press, 1981), 40. See also the discussion of this point in K. Avruch, "Culture and Conflict Resolution," in Avruch, Black, and Scimecca, eds., *Conflict Resolution: Cross-Cultural Perspectives*, 4–7.

144. See Strauss, *Mirrors and Masks*.

145. K-F. Koch, *War and Peace in Jalemo: The Management of Conflict in Highland New Guinea* (Cambridge, Mass.: Harvard University Press, 1974).

146. E. E. Evans-Pritchard, *The Nuer* (Oxford: Oxford University Press, 1940).

147. M. H. Ross, *The Management of Conflict: Interpretations and Interests in Comparative Perspective* (New Haven, Conn.: Yale University Press, 1993), 35–38.

148. For a clear-eyed discussion of these roles, tied to a strongly ethical stance, see Laue and Cormick, "The Ethics of Intervention in Community Disputes." For an outrightly critical view of some third-party roles and processes see, for example, Laura Nader, "Harmony Models and the Construction of Law," in Avruch, Black, and Scimecca, eds., *Conflict Resolution: Cross-Cultural Perspectives*, 41–59; and J. Scimecca, "Conflict Resolution and a Critique of 'Alternative Dispute Resolution,'" in H. Pepinsky and R. Quinney, eds., *Criminology as Peacemaking* (Bloomington: Indiana University Press, 1991), 263–279.

149. It is possible to differentiate arbitrator from adjudicator in the following way: The arbitrator is chosen by the parties, who agree in advance to abide by the rendered decision; in a sense the authority of the arbitrator comes from the parties themselves. In contrast, the adjudicator (for example, the court) can impose itself on the parties and their dispute whether or not they call for it; and the adjudicator possesses an authority structure (police—broadly, the state) that has the power independently to enforce a party's compliance with its decisions. The distinction between mediation and arbitration or adjudication is examined at some length by Gulliver in his *Disputes and Negotiations*.

150. J. Bercovitch, "Thinking about Mediation," in J. Bercovitch, ed., *Resolving International Conflicts: The Theory and Practice of Mediation* (Boulder, Colo.: Lynne Rienner, 1996), 3.

151. The uses (and misuses) of ethnographic descriptions of small-scale, non-Western conflict management processes for the development of alternative dispute resolution (ADR) in the United States are examined in K. Avruch and P. W. Black, "ADR, Palau, and the Contribution of Anthropology," in A. Wolfe and H. Yang, eds., *Anthropological Contributions to Conflict Resolution* (Athens: University of Georgia Press, 1996), 47–63.

152. For a strong statement on the importance of culture addressed to lawyers and adjudication, see S. Merry, "Disputing without Culture," *Harvard Law Review* 100 (1987): 2057–2073.

153. See, for example, R. J. Fisher and L. Keashly, "Distinguishing Third Party Interventions in Intergroup Conflict: Consultation Is *Not* Mediation," *Negotiation Journal* 4, no. 4 (1988): 381–393; L. Kriesberg, "Formal and Quasi-Mediators in International Disputes: An Exploratory Analysis," *Journal of Peace Research* 28, no. 1 (1991): 19–27; and C. R. Mitchell, "The Process and Stages of Mediation: Two Sudanese Cases," in D. Smock, ed., *Making War and Waging Peace: Foreign*

Intervention in Africa (Washington, D.C.: United States Institute of Peace Press, 1993), 139–159.

154. See, for example, P. Salem, "A Critique of Western Conflict Resolution from a Non-Western Perspective," *Negotiation Journal* 9, no. 4 (1993): 361–369.

155. J. P. Lederach, "The North American Mediator's Cultural Assumptions," *Conciliation Quarterly Newsletter* 5 (1986): 2–5.

156. M. Abu-Nimer, "Conflict Resolution Approaches: Western and Middle Eastern Lessons and Possibilities," *American Journal of Economics and Sociology* 55, no. 1 (1996): 35–52; and Abu-Nimer, "Conflict Resolution in an Islamic Context," *Peace and Change* 21, no. 1 (1996): 22–40.

157. S. Merry, *Getting Justice and Getting Even* (Chicago: University of Chicago Press, 1990).

158. P. J. Carnevale and S. Arad, "Bias and Impartiality in International Mediation," in Bercovitch, ed., *Resolving International Conflicts*, 39–74.

159. Avruch, "Conflict Resolution," 241–245.

160. P. Wehr and J. P. Lederach, "Mediating Conflict in Central America," *Journal of Peace Research* 28, no. 1 (1991): 85–98.

161. This is still a matter of some debate; see. J. Mackinlay, ed., *A Guide to Peace Support Operations* (Providence, R.I.: Watson Institute for International Studies, Brown University, 1996), 10–11, 20–21.

162. J. Bercovitch and A. Houston, "The Study of International Mediation: Theoretical Issues and Empirical Evidence," in Bercovitch, ed., *Resolving International Conflicts*, 15–16. Attention to context and other aspects of the interventionary situation, such as conflict phase or stage, is part of the "contingency model," a broader approach to mediation, favored by Bercovitch and Ronald Fisher.

163. Bercovitch, "Thinking about Mediation," 7.

164. For example, it has been referred to as a third-party consultation (Ronald Fisher), controlled communication workshop (early Burton), analytical problem-solving workshop (later Burton, and Christopher Mitchell), and interactive problem-solving workshop (Kelman). Thus far, the most comprehensive treatment of the workshop is found in R. J. Fisher, *Interactive Conflict Resolution* (Syracuse: Syracuse University Press, 1997).

165. Two of the originators of the idea of second-track diplomacy, John McDonald and Joseph Montville, came to it after careers in the U.S. State Department; see, J. W. McDonald and D. B. Bendahmane, *Conflict Resolution: Track Two Diplomacy* (Washington, D.C.: Foreign Service Institute, 1987); and J. V. Montville, "Transnationalism and the Role of Track Two Diplomacy," in W. S. Thompson and K. M. Jensen, eds., *Approaches to Peace: An Intellectual Map* (Washington, D.C.: United States Institute of Peace Press, 1991), 255–269. More recently, the "second track" has been differentiated into as many as nine different "tracks"—business, media, religious actors, human rights, environmental advocates, and so on—and thus one speaks of "multi-track" diplomacy. See L. Diamond and J. McDonald, *Multi-Track Diplomacy: A Systems Guide and Analysis* (Grinnell, Iowa: Iowa Peace Institute, 1991).

166. R. J. Fisher, "Third-Party Consultation as a Method of Intergroup Conflict Resolution: A Review of Studies," *Journal of Conflict Resolution* 27, no. 2 (1983): 301–334.

167. E. Azar, *The Management of Protracted Social Conflict: Theory and Cases* (Brookfield, Vt.: Gower, 1990); J. W. Burton, *Resolving Deep-Rooted Conflicts: A Handbook* (Lanham, Md.: University Press of America, 1987).

168. A partial, brief history of the movement can be found in B. J. Hill, "An Analysis of Conflict Resolution Techniques: From Problem-Solving Workshops to Theory," *Journal of Conflict Resolution* 26, no. 1 (1982), especially 119–129. This history slights the church-related components; on these see, for example, Curle, *Making Peace*, and his *In the Middle: Non-Official Mediation in Violent Situations* (Oxford: Berg, 1986). See also C. H. Yarrow, *Quaker Experiences in International Conciliation* (New Haven, Conn.: Yale University Press, 1972).

169. L. Doob, *Resolving Conflict in Africa: The Fermeda Workshop* (New Haven, Conn.: Yale University Press, 1970); Doob, "A Cyprus Workshop: An Exercise in Intervention Methodology," *Journal of Social Psychology* 94 (1974): 164–178; and Doob and W. J. Foltz, "The Belfast Workshop: An Application of Group Techniques to a Destructive Conflict," *Journal of Conflict Resolution* 17, no. 3 (1973): 489–512. The Belfast (Stirling) Workshop became the object of some controversy, having to do in part with reentry problems experienced by some of the participants; see G. Boehringer, V. Zeruolis, J. Bayley, and K. Boehringer, "Stirling: The Destructive Application of Group Techniques to a Conflict," *Journal of Conflict Resolution* 18, no. 2 (1974): 257–275.

170. This earliest incarnation of the workshop is described in J. W. Burton, *Conflict and Communication: The Use of Controlled Communication in International Relations* (London: Macmillan, 1969).

171. See C. R. Mitchell, *Peacemaking and the Consultant's Role* (Farnborough, England: Gower Press, 1981); and C. R. Mitchell and M. Banks, *Handbook of Conflict Resolution: The Analytical Problem-Solving Approach* (London: Pinter, 1996). We have already mentioned Fisher and Ury's bestselling *Getting to Yes*; see also Fisher's much earlier *International Conflict for Beginners* (New York: Harper and Row, 1969). Herb Kelman has made, since 1972, probably the largest contribution to the literature of these workshops. A good place to get an overview of his work in this area is his chapter in the collection *Managing Global Chaos* (1996); see note 94 above for a sampling and full citations.

172. Burton, *Resolving Deep-Rooted Conflict*, 23.

173. For the longer critique, see Avruch and Black, "A Generic Theory of Conflict Resolution," 87–96, 99–100. For earlier critiques of Burtonian theory and practice, see L. Nader, "Some Notes on John Burton's Paper on 'The Resolution of Conflict,'" *International Studies Quarterly* 16, no. 1 (1972): 53–58; and R. J. Yalem, "Controlled Communication and Conflict Resolution," *Journal of Peace Research* 8, no. 3 (1971): 263–272.

174. See, for example, V. Volkan, J. Montville, and D. Julius, eds., *The Psychodynamics of International Relationships*, 2 vols. (Lexington, Mass.: Lexington Books, 1991).

175. This, indeed, is one way that Burton distinguishes his practice from the bargaining/negotiating practices of, say, Fisher and Ury. The latter do "dig" down beyond surface-level positions to get to interests. But for Burton this is only amateur's archeology: one must excavate beneath interests to values and thence to bedrock—the basic human needs.

176. It is fascinating to think that Burton's insight was reproduced perfectly by President Reagan when he explained to the world, but especially to the Soviets, that the deployment of the Star Wars umbrella, which would protect the United States from Soviet missiles, would also ultimately benefit the Soviets themselves.

177. Burton, *Resolving Deep-Rooted Conflict*, 55.

178. Burton and Dukes, *Conflict*, 200.

179. This section builds upon K. Avruch and P. W. Black, "Conflict Resolution in Intercultural Settings: Problems and Prospects," in D. Sandole and H. van der Merwe, eds., *Conflict Resolution Theory and Practice: Integration and Application* (Manchester, England: Manchester University Press, 1994), 40–41.

180. I. W. Zartman, ed., *The 50% Solution* (New York: Anchor Press/Doubleday, 1976).

181. See Avruch and Black, "Ideas of Human Nature," 221–228.

182. Lederach, *Preparing for Peace*, 81.

183. Both citations are from J. F. Hamill, *Ethno-Logic: The Anthropology of Human Reasoning* (Urbana: University of Illinois Press, 1990), 104.

184. E. Hutchins, *Culture and Inference* (Cambridge, Mass.: Harvard University Press, 1980).

185. D'Andrade, *The Development of Cognitive Anthropology*, 198.

186. Kelman, for example, argues for their ongoing utility. For the contingency view, see L. Keashly and R. J. Fisher, "A Contingency Perspective on Conflict Interventions: Theoretical and Practical Considerations," in Bercovitch, ed., *Resolving International Conflicts*, 235–261; and, in the same volume, L. Kriesberg, "Varieties of Mediating Activities and Mediators in International Relations," 219–233. For an appreciation of the importance of the prenegotiation stage, see H. H. Saunders, "We Need a Larger Theory of Negotiation: The Importance of the Pre-Negotiation Phase," *Negotiation Journal* 1, no. 3 (1985): 249–262. Saunders is a former diplomat who played an important role as a third party in Arab-Israeli, and (as a primary participant) in U.S.-Soviet, negotiations.

187. See Cynthia Sampson, "Religion and Peacebuilding," in Zartman and Rasmussen, eds., *Peacemaking in International Conflict*.

188. One need only compare Burton's 1987 handbook with the handbook, published in 1996, by two of his most active younger collaborators, Mitchell and Banks; for one thing, there are plenty of "scenarios" and open-ended, agreeably complicated "exercises" in the latter work, and not a single Rule. Mitchell and Banks, *Handbook of Conflict Resolution*.

189. Ibid., 6. On this point, see also J. Rothman, *From Confrontation to Cooperation: Resolving Ethnic and Regional Conflict* (Newbury Park, Calif.: Sage, 1992). Rothman describes and analyzes in some depth an Israeli-Palestinian workshop.

190. Lederach, *Preparing for Peace*, 55.

191. Ibid., 51.

192. Kelman and Rouhana, "Promoting Joint Thinking in International Conflicts," 174.

193. Gulliver, *Disputes and Negotiations*.

194. Ross, *The Management of Conflict*, 180.

195. Kelman and Rouhana, "Promoting Joint Thinking in International Conflicts," 174.

196. The question of what constitutes a "successful" workshop—indeed, the whole issue of the assessment of this technique—is formidable, as friendly critics and committed practitioners all agree; see, for example, Fisher, "Third Party Consultation as a Method of Intergroup Conflict Resolution"; Hill, "An Analysis of Conflict Resolution Techniques"; and Mitchell and Banks, *Handbook of Conflict Resolution*, 148–157. Many of the methodological obstacles are dictated by the strict requirements of confidentiality (if not secrecy) in the process and by limited data collection and distribution. Even granted this, the effects would be hard to measure, since conflict transformation, even when it occurs, is likely to be gradual and incremental, not cataclysmic. Still, there have been not insignificant indirect measures of at least influence, if not wholesale transformation. The most convincing comes from Kelman's ongoing Israeli-Palestinian workshops. He notes that many of the Israeli and Palestinian interlocutors since 1991 had also been participants in the workshops, and moreover that many "alumni" of the workshops "can now be found in the Israeli cabinet, Knesset, and foreign ministry, as well as in leading positions in various Palestinian agencies" (Kelman, "The Interactive Problem-Solving Approach," 509). The most balanced treatment of assessment may be found in Fisher's *Interactive Conflict Resolution*, 187–212. When all is said, however, the problem of assessing outcomes with a rigor amenable to most behavioral scientists, and not a few policymakers, is likely to remain with us.

197. It is for Lederach a transformation toward "building" peace; see also his *Building Peace: Sustainable Reconciliation in Divided Societies*, 2d ed. (Washington, D.C.: United States Institute of Peace Press, 1997).

198. The evolution of this position is very evident in John Burton's work, because he has been laboring in these fields for so long. In the late 1960s Burton saw his workshops and conflict resolution in the narrow terms of "controlled communication processes." By the late 1980s he was writing about "conflict resolution as a political system."

199. J. Scimecca, "Conflict Resolution in the United States: The Emergence of a Profession?" in Avruch, Black, and Scimecca, eds., *Conflict Resolution: Cross-Cultural Perspectives*, 19–39.

200. R. E. Rubenstein, "Dispute Resolution on the Eastern Frontier: Some Questions for Modern Missionaries," *Negotiation Journal* 8, no. 3 (1992): 205–213.

201. R. Fisher, E. Kopelman, and A. K. Schneider, *Beyond Machiavelli: Tools for Coping with Conflict* (New York: Penguin Books, 1996), 4–5.

202. R. Cohen, "An Advocate's View," in Faure and Rubin, eds., *Culture and Negotiation*, 35–36.

203. D'Andrade, *The Development of Cognitive Anthropology*, 249.

204. F. G. Bailey, "*Tertius Luctans*: Idiocosm, Caricature, and Mask," in Avruch, Black, and Scimecca, eds., *Conflict Resolution: Cross-Cultural Perspectives*, 82.

Bibliography

Abu-Nimer, M. "Conflict Resolution Approaches: Western and Middle Eastern Lessons and Possibilities." *American Journal of Economics and Sociology* 55, no. 1 (1996): 35–52.

———. "Conflict Resolution in an Islamic Context." *Peace and Change* 21, no. 1 (1996): 22–40.

Agar, M. *Language Shock*. New York: Morrow, 1994.

Almond, G. "Comparative Political Systems." *Journal of Politics* 18 (1956): 391–409.

Almond, G., and S. Verba., eds. *The Civic Culture: Political Attitudes and Democracy in Five Nations*. Princeton, N.J.: Princeton University Press, 1963.

Avruch, K. "Conflict Resolution." *Encyclopedia of Cultural Anthropology*. Vol. 1. New York: Henry Holt, 1996.

———. "Culture and Conflict Resolution." In K. Avruch, P. W. Black, and J. Scimecca, eds., *Conflict Resolution: Cross-Cultural Perspectives*. New York: Greenwood Press, 1991.

———. "Making Culture and Its Costs." *Ethnic and Racial Studies* 15, no. 4 (1992): 614–626.

Avruch, K., and P. W. Black. "ADR, Palau, and the Contribution of Anthropology." In A. Wolfe and H. Yang, eds., *Anthropological Contributions to Conflict Resolution*. Athens: University of Georgia Press, 1996.

———. "Conflict Resolution in Intercultural Settings: Problems and Prospects." In D. Sandole and H. van der Merwe, eds., *Conflict Resolution Theory and Practice: Integration and Application*. Manchester, England: Manchester University Press, 1994.

————. "The Culture Question and Conflict Resolution." *Peace and Change* 16, no. 1 (1991): 22–45.

————. "A Generic Theory of Conflict Resolution: A Critique." *Negotiation Journal* 3, no. 1 (1987): 87–96, 99–100.

————. "Ideas of Human Nature in Contemporary Conflict Resolution Theory." *Negotiation Journal* 6, no. 3 (1990): 221–228.

Avruch, K.; P. W. Black; and J. Scimecca, eds. *Conflict Resolution: Cross-Cultural Perspectives.* New York: Greenwood Press, 1991.

Azar, E. *The Management of Protracted Social Conflict: Theory and Cases.* Brookfield, Vt.: Gower, 1990.

Bailey, F. G. "*Tertius Luctans*: Idiocosm, Caricature, and Mask." In K. Avruch, P. W. Black, and J. Scimecca, eds., *Conflict Resolution: Cross-Cultural Perspectives.* New York: Greenwood Press, 1991.

Banks, M. "The International Relations Discipline: Asset or Liability for Conflict Resolution?" In E. Azar and J. Burton, eds., *International Conflict Resolution: Theory and Practice.* Sussex, England: Wheatsheaf, 1986.

Beeman, W. "Conflict and Belief in American Foreign Policy." In M. L. Foster and R. A. Rubinstein, eds., *Peace and War: Cross-Cultural Perspectives.* New Brunswick, N.J.: Transaction Books, 1986.

Begin, M. *The Revolt.* New York: Nash, 1977.

Ben-Yehuda, N. *The Masada Myth: Collective Memory and Mythmaking in Israel.* Madison: University of Wisconsin Press, 1995.

Benedict, R. *The Chrysanthemum and the Sword.* Boston: Houghton Mifflin, 1946.

————. *Patterns of Culture.* New York: Houghton Mifflin, 1934.

Bercovitch, J. "Thinking about Mediation." In J. Bercovitch, ed., *Resolving International Conflicts: The Theory and Practice of Mediation.* Boulder, Colo.: Lynne Rienner, 1996.

Bercovitch, J., and A. Houston. "The Study of International Mediation: Theoretical Issues and Empirical Evidence." In J. Bercovitch, ed., *Resolving International Conflicts: The Theory and Practice of Mediation.* Boulder, Colo.: Lynne Rienner, 1996.

Bernstein, B. "Elaborated and Restricted Codes: Their Social Origins and Consequences." In J. Gumperz and D. Hymes, eds., "The Ethnography of Communication," *American Anthropologist* 66, no. 6, pt. 2 (1964): 55–69.

Berridge, G. R. *Diplomacy: Theory and Practice.* New York: Prentice Hall, 1995.

Binnendijk, H., ed. *National Negotiating Styles.* Washington, D.C.: Foreign Service Institute, U.S. Department of State, 1987.

Black, P. W., and K. Avruch. "Culture, Power, and International Negotiations: Understanding Palau-U.S. Status Negotiations." *Millennium: Journal of International Studies* 22, no. 3 (1993): 379–400.

———. "Some Issues in Thinking about Culture and the Resolution of Conflict." *Humanity and Society* 13, no. 1 (1989): 187–194.

Blake, R. R., and J. S. Mouton. *The Managerial Grid.* Houston: Gulf Publishing, 1964.

Blaker, M. *Japanese International Negotiating Style.* New York: Columbia University Press, 1977.

Boehringer, G.; V. Zeruolis; J. Bayley; and K. Boehringer. "Stirling: The Destructive Application of Group Techniques to a Conflict." *Journal of Conflict Resolution* 18, no. 2 (1974): 257–275.

Boulding, K. *Three Faces of Power.* Beverly Hills, Calif.: Sage, 1989.

Bourdieu, P. *The Logic of Practice.* Stanford, Calif.: Stanford University Press, 1990.

———. *Outline of a Theory of Practice.* Cambridge: Cambridge University Press, 1977.

Boyd, R., and P. Richerson. *Culture and Evolutionary Process.* Chicago: University of Chicago Press, 1985.

Burton, J. W. *Conflict and Communication: The Use of Controlled Communication in International Relations.* London: Macmillan, 1969.

———. *Conflict: Resolution and Provention.* New York: St. Martin's, 1990.

———. *Resolving Deep-Rooted Conflicts: A Handbook.* Lanham, Md.: University Press of America, 1987.

Burton, J. W., and F. Dukes. *Conflict: Practices in Management, Settlement, and Resolution.* New York: St. Martin's, 1990.

Carnevale, P. J., and S. Arad. "Bias and Impartiality in International Mediation." In J. Bercovitch, ed., *Resolving International Conflicts: The Theory and Practice of Mediation.* Boulder, Colo.: Lynne Rienner, 1996.

Carr, E. H. *The Twenty Years' Crisis, 1919–1939.* 1939. Reprint, New York: Harper and Row, 1964.

Chilton, P. *Security Metaphors: Cold War Discourse from Containment to Common House.* New York: Peter Lang, 1996.

Cohen, R. "An Advocate's View." In G. Faure and J. Rubin, eds., *Culture and Negotiation.* Newbury Park, Calif.: Sage, 1993.

———. *Culture and Conflict in Egyptian-Israeli Relations: A Dialogue of the Deaf.* Bloomington: Indiana University Press, 1990.

————. *Negotiating across Cultures: Communication Obstacles in International Diplomacy.* Washington, D.C.: United States Institute of Peace Press, 1991.

Comaroff, J., and S. Roberts. *Rules and Processes: The Cultural Context of Dispute in an African Context.* Chicago: University of Chicago Press, 1981.

Coser, L. *The Functions of Social Conflict.* New York: Free Press, 1956.

Curle, A. *In the Middle: Non-Official Mediation in Violent Situations.* Oxford: Berg, 1986.

————. *Making Peace.* London: Tavistock, 1971.

D'Andrade, R. *The Development of Cognitive Anthropology.* Cambridge: Cambridge University Press, 1995.

Diamond, L., and J. McDonald. *Multi-Track Diplomacy: A Systems Guide and Analysis.* Grinnell, Iowa: Iowa Peace Institute, 1991.

Doob, L. "A Cyprus Workshop: An Exercise in Intervention Methodology." *Journal of Social Psychology* 94 (1974): 164–178.

————. *Resolving Conflict in Africa: The Fermeda Workshop.* New Haven, Conn.: Yale University Press, 1970.

Doob, L., and W. J. Foltz. "The Belfast Workshop: An Application of Group Techniques to a Destructive Conflict." *Journal of Conflict Resolution* 17, no. 3 (1973): 489–512.

Douglas, M. *Natural Symbols: Explorations in Cosmology.* 2d ed. London: Routledge, 1996.

Douglas, M., and A. Wildavsky. *Risk and Culture: An Essay on the Selection of Technological and Environmental Dangers.* Berkeley: University of California Press, 1982.

Druckman, D., ed. *Negotiations: Social-Psychological Perspectives.* Beverly Hills, Calif.: Sage, 1977.

Druckman, D.; A. Benton; F. Ali; and J. Bagur. "Cultural Differences in Bargaining Behavior: India, Argentina, and the United States." *Journal of Conflict Resolution* 20, no. 3 (1976): 413–452.

Evans-Pritchard, E. E. *The Nuer.* Oxford: Oxford University Press, 1940.

Faure, G., and J. Rubin. "Lessons for Theory and Research." In G. Faure and J. Rubin, eds., *Culture and Negotiation.* Newbury Park, Calif.: Sage, 1993.

Fernandez, J., ed. *Beyond Metaphor: The Theory of Tropes in Anthropology.* Stanford, Calif.: Stanford University Press, 1991.

Fisher, G. *International Negotiation: A Cross-Cultural Perspective.* Yarmouth, Maine: Intercultural Press, 1980.

————. *Mindsets: The Role of Culture and Perception in International Relations.* Yarmouth, Maine: Intercultural Press, 1988.

Fisher, R. *International Conflict for Beginners*. New York: Harper and Row, 1969.

Fisher, R., and W. Ury. *Getting to Yes*. Boston: Houghton Mifflin, 1981.

Fisher, R.; W. Ury; and B. Patton. *Getting to Yes*. 2d ed. Boston: Houghton Mifflin, 1991.

Fisher, R.; E. Kopelman; and A. K. Schneider. *Beyond Machiavelli: Tools for Coping with Conflict*. New York: Penguin Books, 1996.

Fisher, R. J. *Interactive Conflict Resolution*. Syracuse: Syracuse University Press, 1997.

———. "Third Party Consultation as a Method of Intergroup Conflict Resolution: A Review of Studies." *Journal of Conflict Resolution* 27, no. 2 (1983): 301–334.

Fisher, R. J., and L. Keashly. "Distinguishing Third Party Interventions in Intergroup Conflict: Consultation Is *Not* Mediation." *Negotiation Journal* 4, no. 4 (1988): 381–393.

Fox, R. G., ed. *Nationalist Ideologies and the Production of National Cultures*. Washington, D.C.: American Anthropological Association, 1990.

Freeman, C. Jr., ed. *The Diplomat's Dictionary*. Washington, D.C.: National Defense University Press, 1994.

Galtung, J. "Violence, Peace, and Peace Research." *Journal of Peace Research* 6, no. 3 (1969): 167–191.

Geertz, C. *The Interpretation of Cultures*. New York: Basic Books, 1973.

———. *Local Knowledge: Further Essays in Interpretive Anthropology*. New York: Basic Books, 1983.

———. *Works and Lives: The Anthropologist as Author*. Stanford, Calif.: Stanford University Press, 1988.

George, A. *Bridging the Gap: Theory and Practice in Foreign Policy*. Washington, D.C.: United States Institute of Peace Press, 1993.

———. *Forceful Persuasion: Coercive Diplomacy as an Alternative to War*. Washington, D.C.: United States Institute of Peace Press, 1991.

Giddens, A. *The Constitution of Society*. Cambridge: Polity Press, 1984.

Glenn, E. *Man and Mankind: Conflict and Communication between Cultures*. Norwood, N.J.: Ablex, 1981.

Goffman, E. *Asylums*. Chicago: Aldine, 1962.

Greenhouse, C. *Praying for Justice: Faith, Order, and Community in an American Town*. Ithaca, N.Y.: Cornell University Press, 1986.

Gulliver, P. H. *Disputes and Negotiations: A Cross-Cultural Perspective*. New York: Academic Press, 1979.

Hall, E. T. *Beyond Culture*. New York: Anchor Books, 1976.

————. *The Silent Language*. New York: Doubleday, 1959.

Hall, W. *Managing Cultures: Making Strategic Relationships Work*. New York: Wiley, 1995.

Hamill, J. F. *Ethno-Logic: The Anthropology of Human Reasoning*. Urbana: University of Illinois Press, 1990.

Harkabi, Y. *The Bar Kokhba Syndrome: Risk and Realism in International Relations*. New York: Rossel Books, 1982.

Harris, P., and R. Moran. *Managing Cultural Differences*. 4th ed. Houston: Gulf Publishing, 1996.

Hill, B. J. "An Analysis of Conflict Resolution Techniques: From Problem-Solving Workshops to Theory." *Journal of Conflict Resolution* 26, no. 1 (1982): 109–138.

Hirsch, E. D., Jr.; J. Kett; and J. Trefil, eds. *The Dictionary of Cultural Literacy*. Boston: Houghton Mifflin, 1988.

————. *A First Dictionary of Cultural Literacy: What Our Children Need to Know*. Boston: Houghton Mifflin, 1989.

Hofstede, G. *Culture's Consequences: International Differences in Work-Related Values*. Beverly Hills, Calif.: Sage, 1980.

————. *Cultures and Organizations: Software of the Mind*. New York: McGraw-Hill, 1991.

Hopmann, P. T. *The Negotiation Process and the Resolution of International Conflicts*. Columbia: University of South Carolina Press, 1996.

Huntington, S. *The Clash of Civilizations and the Remaking of World Order*. New York: Simon and Schuster, 1996.

Hutchins, E. *Culture and Inference*. Cambridge, Mass.: Harvard University Press, 1980.

Hybel, A. R. *Power over Rationality: The Bush Administration and the Gulf Crisis*. Albany: State University of New York Press, 1993.

Iklé, F. *How Nations Negotiate*. New York: Harper and Row, 1964.

Jabri, V. *Discourses on Violence: Conflict Analysis Reconsidered*. Manchester, England: Manchester University Press, 1996.

Jervis, R. *Perception and Misperception in International Politics*. Princeton, N.J.: Princeton University Press, 1976.

Johnston, A. "Thinking about Strategic Culture." *International Security* 19, no. 4 (1995): 32–64.

Jonsson, C. *Communication in International Bargaining*. New York: St. Martin's, 1990.

Katriel, T. *Talking Straight: "Dugri" Speech in Israeli Sabra Culture*. Cambridge: Cambridge University Press, 1986.

Keashly, L., and R. J. Fisher. "A Contingency Perspective on Conflict Interventions: Theoretical and Practical Considerations." In J. Bercovitch, ed., *Resolving International Conflicts: The Theory and Practice of Mediation.* Boulder, Colo.: Lynne Rienner, 1996.

Kelman, H. "Informal Mediation by the Scholar/Practitioner." In J. Bercovitch and J. Rubin, eds., *Mediation in International Relations: Multiple Approaches to Conflict Management.* New York: St. Martin's, 1992.

———. "The Interactive Problem-Solving Approach." In C. Crocker, F. Hampson, and P. Aall, eds., *Managing Global Chaos.* Washington, D.C.: United States Institute of Peace Press, 1996.

———. "The Problem-Solving Workshop in Conflict Resolution." In R. Merritt, ed., *Communication in International Politics.* Urbana: University of Illinois Press, 1972.

Kelman, H., and N. Rouhana. "Promoting Joint Thinking in International Conflicts: An Israeli-Palestinian Continuing Workshop." *Journal of Social Issues* 50, no. 1 (1994): 157–178.

Kimmel, P. "Cultural Perspectives on International Negotiations." *Journal of Social Issues* 50, no. 1 (1994): 179–196.

Koch, K-F. *War and Peace in Jalemo: The Management of Conflict in Highland New Guinea.* Cambridge, Mass.: Harvard University Press, 1974.

Kochman, T. *Black and White Styles in Conflict.* Chicago: University of Chicago Press, 1981.

Kriesberg, L. "Conflict Resolution Applications to Peace Studies." *Peace and Change* 16, no. 4 (1991): 400–417.

———. "The Development of the Conflict Resolution Field." In I. W. Zartman and L. Rasmussen, eds., *Peacemaking in International Conflict: Methods and Techniques.* Washington, D.C.: United States Institute of Peace Press, 1997.

———. "Formal and Quasi-Mediators in International Disputes: An Exploratory Analysis." *Journal of Peace Research* 28, no. 1 (1991): 19–27.

———. "Varieties of Mediating Activities and Mediators in International Relations." In J. Bercovitch, ed., *Resolving International Conflicts: The Theory and Practice of Mediation.* Boulder, Colo.: Lynne Rienner, 1996.

Kroeber, A. L., and C. Kluckhohn. *Culture: A Critical Review of Concepts and Definitions.* Papers of the Peabody Museum of American Archaeology and Ethnology, vol. 47. Harvard University, 1952.

Lakoff, G. *Women, Fire, and Dangerous Things*. Chicago: University of Chicago Press, 1987.

Lakoff, G., and M. Johnson. *Metaphors We Live By*. Chicago: University of Chicago Press, 1980.

Lang, W. "A Professional's View." In G. Faure and J. Rubin, eds., *Culture and Negotiation*. Newbury Park, Calif.: Sage, 1993.

Laue, J. "The Emergence and Institutionalization of Third Party Roles in Conflict." In D. Sandole and I. Sandole-Staroste, eds., *Conflict Management and Problem Solving*. New York: New York University Press, 1987.

Laue, J., and G. Cormick. "The Ethics of Intervention in Community Disputes." In G. Bermant, H. Kelman, and D. Warwick, eds., *The Ethics of Social Intervention*. Washington, D.C.: Halstead Press, 1978.

Lederach, J. P. *Building Peace: Sustainable Reconciliation in Divided Societies*. 2d ed. Washington, D.C.: United States Institute of Peace Press, 1997.

———. "The North American Mediator's Cultural Assumptions." *Conciliation Quarterly Newsletter* 5 (1986): 2–5.

———. *Preparing for Peace: Conflict Transformation across Cultures*. Syracuse: Syracuse University Press, 1995.

Lustick, I. *For the Land and the Lord: Jewish Fundamentalism in Israel*. New York: Council on Foreign Relations, 1988.

Lutz, C., and L. Abu-Lughod. *Language and the Politics of Emotion*. New York: Cambridge University Press, 1990.

Mackinlay, J., ed. *A Guide to Peace Support Operations*. Providence, R.I.: Watson Institute for International Studies, Brown University, 1996.

McDonald, J. W., and D. B. Bendahmane. *Conflict Resolution: Track Two Diplomacy*. Washington, D.C.: Foreign Service Institute, 1987.

Merry, S. "Disputing without Culture." *Harvard Law Review* 100 (1987): 2057–2073.

———. *Getting Justice and Getting Even*. Chicago: University of Chicago Press, 1990.

Mitchell, C. R. *Peacemaking and the Consultant's Role*. Farnborough, England: Gower Press, 1981.

———. "The Process and Stages of Mediation: Two Sudanese Cases." In D. Smock, ed., *Making War and Waging Peace: Foreign Intervention in Africa*. Washington, D.C.: United States Institute of Peace Press, 1993.

Mitchell, C. R., and M. Banks. *Handbook of Conflict Resolution: The Analytical Problem-Solving Approach*. London: Pinter, 1996.

Montville, J. V. "Transnationalism and the Role of Track Two Diplomacy." In W. S. Thompson and K. M. Jensen, eds., *Approaches to Peace: An Intellectual Map*. Washington, D.C.: United States Institute of Peace Press, 1991.

Morgenthau, H. *Politics among Nations: The Struggle for Power and Peace*. New York: Knopf, 1956.

Morgenthau, H., and K. W. Thompson. *Politics among Nations: The Struggle for Power and Peace*. 6th ed. New York: Knopf, 1985.

Nader, L. "Harmony Models and the Construction of Law." In K. Avruch, P. W. Black, and J. Scimecca, eds., *Conflict Resolution: Cross-Cultural Perspectives*. New York: Greenwood Press, 1991.

———. "Some Notes on John Burton's Paper on 'The Resolution of Conflict.'" *International Studies Quarterly* 16, no. 1 (1972): 53–58.

Nicolson, H. *Diplomacy*. 3d ed. Oxford: Oxford University Press, 1963.

Nudler, O. "On Conflicts and Metaphors: Towards an Extended Rationality." In J. Burton, ed., *Conflict: Human Needs Theory*. New York: St Martin's, 1990.

Pruitt, D. *Negotiation Behavior*. New York: Academic Press, 1981.

Pruitt, D., and P. Carnevale. *Negotiation in Social Conflict*. Pacific Grove, Calif.: Brooks/Cole, 1993.

Pruitt, D., and J. Rubin. *Social Conflict* New York: Random House, 1986.

Pye, L. *Chinese Commercial Negotiating Style*. Cambridge, Mass.: Oelgeschlager, Gunn and Hain, 1982.

Pye, L., and S. Verba, eds. *Political Culture and Political Development*. Princeton, N.J.: Princeton University Press, 1963.

Pyne, R. J. *The Clash with Distant Cultures*. Albany: State University of New York Press, 1995.

Quandt, W. B. "Egypt: A Strong Sense of National Identity." In H. Binnendijk, ed., *National Negotiating Styles*. Washington, D.C.: Foreign Service Institute, U.S. Department of State, 1987.

Raiffa, H. *The Art and Science of Negotiation*. Cambridge, Mass.: Harvard University Press, 1982.

Rapoport, A. *Fights, Games, and Debates*. Ann Arbor: University of Michigan Press, 1960.

Reed, S. *Making Common Sense of Japan*. Pittsburgh: University of Pittsburgh Press, 1993.

Rohlen, T. *For Harmony and Strength*. Berkeley: University of California Press, 1974.

Rosenau, J. N. *Turbulence in World Politics: A Theory of Change and Continuity*. Princeton, N.J.: Princeton University Press, 1990.

Ross, M. H. *The Management of Conflict: Interpretations and Interests in Comparative Perspective*. New Haven, Conn.: Yale University Press, 1993.

Rothman, J. *From Confrontation to Cooperation: Resolving Ethnic and Regional Conflict*. Newbury Park, Calif.: Sage, 1992.

Rubenstein, R. E. "Dispute Resolution on the Eastern Frontier: Some Questions for Modern Missionaries." *Negotiation Journal* 8, no. 3 (1992): 205–213.

Rubin, J.; D. Pruitt; and S. Kim. *Social Conflict: Escalation, Stalemate, and Settlement*. 2d ed. New York: McGraw-Hill, 1994.

Rubinstein, R. A. "Cultural Analysis and International Security." *Alternatives* 13, no. 4 (1988): 529–542.

———. "Culture, International Affairs, and Multilateral Peacekeeping: Confusing Process and Pattern." *Cultural Dynamics* 2, no. 1 (1989): 41–61.

Salem, P. "A Critique of Western Conflict Resolution from a Non-Western Perspective." *Negotiation Journal* 9, no. 4 (1993): 361–369.

Sampson, C. "Religion and Peacebuilding." In I. W. Zartman and L. Rasmussen, eds., *Peacemaking in International Conflict: Methods and Techniques*. Washington, D.C.: United States Institute of Peace Press, 1997.

Saunders, H. H. "We Need a Larger Theory of Negotiation: The Importance of the Pre-Negotiation Phase." *Negotiation Journal* 1, no. 3 (1985): 249–262.

Schelling, T. *The Strategy of Conflict*. 1960. Reprint, Cambridge, Mass.: Harvard University Press, 1980.

Schwartz, T. "Anthropology and Psychology: An Unrequited Relationship." In T. Schwartz, G. White, and C. Lutz, eds., *New Directions in Psychological Anthropology*. Cambridge: Cambridge University Press, 1992.

Scimecca, J. "Conflict Resolution and a Critique of 'Alternative Dispute Resolution.'" In H. Pepinsky and R. Quinney, eds., *Criminology as Peacemaking*. Bloomington: Indiana University Press, 1991.

———. "Conflict Resolution in the United States: The Emergence of a Profession?" In K. Avruch, P. W. Black, and J. Scimecca, eds., *Conflict Resolution: Cross-Cultural Perspectives*. New York: Greenwood Press, 1991.

Smith, R. F. *Negotiating with the Soviets*. Bloomington: Indiana University Press, 1989.

Solomon, R. H. *Chinese Political Negotiating Behavior, 1967–1984*. Santa Monica, Calif.: RAND Corporation, 1995.

Spiro, M. "Collective Representations and Mental Representations in Religious Symbol Systems." In B. Kilborn and L. Langness, eds., *Culture and Human Nature: The Theoretical Papers of Melford E. Spiro*. Chicago: University of Chicago Press, 1987.

Strauss, A. *Mirrors and Masks*. Glencoe, Ill.: Free Press, 1959.

Sunshine, R. *Negotiating for International Development: A Practitioner's Handbook*. Dordrecht, The Netherlands: Martinus Nijhoff, 1990.

Tuchman, B. *The March of Folly*. New York: Ballantine, 1985.

Tylor, E. *Primitive Culture*. 1870. Reprint, New York: Harper and Row, 1958.

Vasquez, J. *The War Puzzle*. Cambridge: Cambridge University Press, 1993.

Vlahos, M. "Culture and Foreign Policy." *Foreign Policy* 82 (spring 1991): 59–78.

Volkan, V.; J. Montville; and D. Julius. *The Psychodynamics of International Relationships*. Vol. 1, *Concepts and Theories*. Lexington, Mass.: Lexington Books, 1991.

———. *The Psychodynamics of International Relationships*. Vol. 2, *Unofficial Diplomacy at Work*. Lexington, Mass.: Lexington Books, 1991.

von Neumann, J., and O. Morgenstern. *Theory of Games and Economic Behavior*. Princeton, N.J.: Princeton University Press, 1944.

Walton, R., and R. McKersie. *A Behavioral Theory of Labor Negotiations*. New York: McGraw-Hill, 1965.

Weaver, G. *Culture, Communication, and Conflict*. Needham Heights, Mass.: Ginn Press, 1994.

Wehr, P. *Conflict Regulation*. Boulder, Colo.: Westview Press, 1979.

Wehr, P., and J. P. Lederach. "Mediating Conflict in Central America." *Journal of Peace Research* 28, no. 1 (1991): 85–98.

Weiss, S. "Negotiating with Romans, Part I." *Sloan Management Review* 35, no. 2 (1994): 51–61.

Wendt, A. "Constructing International Politics." *International Security* 20, no. 1 (1995): 71–81.

White, R. K. *Nobody Wanted War: Misperception in Vietnam and Other Wars*. Rev. ed. New York: Doubleday, 1970.

Wildavsky, A. "Change in Political Culture." *Politics* 20, no. 2 (1985): 95–102.

Williams, R. *Keywords*. New York: Oxford University Press, 1983.

Wolf, E. "Facing Power: Old Insights, New Questions." *American Anthropologist* 92, no. 3 (1990): 586–596.

Yalem, R. J. "Controlled Communication and Conflict Resolution." *Journal of Peace Research* 8, no. 3 (1971): 263–272.

Yarrow, C. H. *Quaker Experiences in International Conciliation.* New Haven, Conn.: Yale University Press, 1972.

Zartman, I. W. "A Skeptic's View." In G. Faure and J. Rubin, eds., *Culture and Negotiation.* Newbury Park, Calif.: Sage, 1993.

Zartman, I. W., ed. *The 50% Solution.* New York: Anchor Press/Doubleday, 1976.

Zartman, I. W., and M. Berman. *The Practical Negotiator.* New York: Yale University Press, 1982.

Zerubavel, Y. *Recovered Roots: Collective Memory and the Making of Israeli National Tradition.* Chicago: University of Chicago Press, 1995.

Index

Abu-Nimer, Mohammed, 83, 84
actors, situated, 38, 56
adjudicator, 82, 89
    distinguished from arbitrator,
        124 n. 149
    see also arbitrator
ADR. *See* dispute, resolution,
    alternative
Afghanistan, 30, 50
African Americans, 78–79
Agar, M., 111 n. 16
Almond, Gabriel, 31
Alternative Dispute Resolution.
    See dispute, resolution
amae, 61, 63
anthropology
    analysis in, 61
    and the concept of culture,
        11, 110 n. 11
    legacy of, 31
    legal, on conflict manage-
        ment, 82
Arabs, 15–16, 71–72, 121–122
    nn. 123, 128
arbitration, uses of, 82, 86
arbitrator
    distinguished from adjudica-
        tor, 124 n. 149

arbitrator *(cont.)*
    distinguished from mediator,
        81–82
Arnold, Matthew, 6, 7–8, 9, 12,
    16
Avruch, Kevin, 10, 63, 97
Azar, Edward, 86
Aziz, Tariq, 48

Bailey, F. G., 108
Baker, James, 48
balance of power. *See* power
Bali, cock fighting in, 61, 62
Banks, Michael, 87, 95, 96
bargaining
    game theory and, 76–78
    unacceptability of, as conflict
        resolution, 26, 102
bedu, 61
behavior, and game theory, 74–76
Belgium, 30
belief (and perception), as
        causes of conflict, 23, 27,
        35, 38, 57, 100
    see also cognitivism;
        misperception
Benedict, Ruth, 8, 11, 12, 32,
        33, 34, 61, 110 n. 12

Kevin Avruch is professor of anthropology, an affiliated faculty member of the Institute for Conflict Analysis and Resolution, and a senior fellow in the Program on Peacekeeping Policy, at George Mason University. He is the author of *American Immigrants in Israel: Social Identities and Change*, and co-editor of *Conflict Resolution: Cross-Cultural Perspectives* and *Critical Essays on Israeli Society, Religion, and Government*. He was a 1996–97 senior fellow in the Jennings Randolph Program for International Peace at the United States Institute of Peace.

JENNINGS RANDOLPH PROGRAM FOR INTERNATIONAL PEACE

This book is a fine example of the work produced by senior fellows in the Jennings Randolph fellowship program of the United States Institute of Peace. As part of the statute establishing the Institute, Congress envisioned a program that would appoint "scholars and leaders of peace from the United States and abroad to pursue scholarly inquiry and other appropriate forms of communication on international peace and conflict resolution." The program was named after Senator Jennings Randolph of West Virginia, whose efforts over four decades helped to establish the Institute.

Since 1987, the Jennings Randolph Program has played a key role in the Institute's effort to build a national center of research, dialogue, and education on critical problems of conflict and peace. More than a hundred senior fellows from some thirty nations have carried out projects on the sources and nature of violent international conflict and the ways such conflict can be peacefully managed or resolved. Fellows come from a wide variety of academic and other professional backgrounds. They conduct research at the Institute and participate in the Institute's outreach activities to policymakers, the academic community, and the American public.

Each year approximately fifteen senior fellows are in residence at the Institute. Fellowship recipients are selected by the Institute's board of directors in a competitive process. For further information on the program, or to receive an application form, please contact the program staff at (202) 457-1700.

Joseph Klaits
Director

Culture and Conflict Resolution

This book is set in Goudy; the display type is Twentieth Century. Hasten Design Studio designed the book's cover, and Joan Engelhardt and Day Dosch designed the interior. Pages were made up by Day Dosch. The book's editor was Nigel Quinney.